It is
what
it is

It is what it is

Learning to LIVE with my BRAIN TUMOR

JULIE SAEGER NIERENBERG

Printed in the United States of America.

ISBN
979-8-88945-131-0 (Paperback)
979-8-88945-132-7 (Ebook)
979-8-88945-133-4 (Hardback)

Brilliant Books Literary
137 Forest Park Lane Thomasville
North Carolina 27360 USA

"The beginning of wisdom comes from the capacity to look at what is."

- Ram Dass[1]

---

[1] Reprinted with permission from RamDass/RamDass.org

"The real battle is with our own inner feelings and beliefs about how it ought to be."

- Ram Dass[2]

TABLE OF CONTENTS

DEDICATION

I dedicate these pages to all who helped me through the many moments of discovery, deliberation and decision-making. You shower me with abundant gifts of spirit, positivity, prayer and patience. I am lifted and loved.

Gratitude for my family and dear friends, who make certain I feel supported at every turn, is my constant companion.

Kerry and Valerie, my precious daughters, you infuse me with new life with every breath I take. You have done so since your conception.

Earl, my Beloved, thank you for holding my heart as you hold my hand.

My vision for the future is filled with the memories we'll create, the joys we'll share and treasure. I intend to grow very old, so be ready to put up with me.

It is what it is, and
the best is yet to be.

1

The Brain Scan

This is exactly how I found out.

"You have masses in your brain," said the doctor who had called me in. Substituting for my own doctor, she was proactively taking steps to care for me and move my case forward, while my own physician was out of office all week. She conducted visual clarity and visual range tests.

I wondered: Were the brain masses lurking near my optical processing centers, prompting these tests?

"Wow, I thought it would be a sinus issue!" was my reply. And I still thought so. *Couldn't you be wrong about the brain masses?* This is what denial feels like. *Brain masses?* Who knew? I've had headaches, cranial-facial pressure and some other sinus-seeming symptoms. "I'm just sure I have sinusitis . . ."

"The MRI shows that you have masses, tissue of an unknown type, and in places in your brain that may contribute to some of the problems you're experiencing."

After asking her many questions, which she declined to answer, responsibly citing her lack of knowledge and the somewhat vague nature of the MRI (magnetic resonance imaging) scan report, I requested a copy of that same report. She would not share it with me, saying the neurosurgeon would be better equipped to comment on it and to order the best tests for this preliminary stage. Now I really wondered what that report said . . .

The reassuring things she had to say were: 1) we found it now before any further growth and 2) the radiologist's report said it did not look like "cancerous" masses. Their true nature, source and treatment are all in the category of unknown until further diagnostic work is done under the neurosurgeon's pending care.

I asked about alien digital programming implants and Star Trek-ian otherworldly brain worms as possibilities for these masses of unknown origin, but the doctor's sense of humor wasn't as desperately creative as mine. I barely got a smile.

And so went our short visit. The substitute general practitioner sent an urgent referral to a neurosurgeon and I entered a waiting pattern of unknown duration.

I left the doctor's office. On the stairwell, I felt an initial surge of tears, but they didn't come through. I thought about crying, but I didn't *feel* like doing so. Driving home I was most concerned about my husband, my life partner, my beloved, who would soon be hearing me break this news as gently and reassuringly as possible.

And so, I did my best to do that. I gently told him what I hadn't yet accepted myself.

At first, he thought I must be joking. But he soon realized I was not. This was not joking material, despite my attempt to do so with the stand-in doctor. After explaining all to my husband Earl to the best of my limited knowledge and ability, he so tenderly said to me, "We'll get through this together. I love you."

2

Saying My Peace: A Midsummer Night's Enlightening Bolt

Kaboom! From a deep sleep, I bolted upright with a lightning jolt sensation. A particular message just had to be downloaded in my brain from the status of "intuitive sense" to one of "full conscious awareness" at that particular moment: 4 a.m.

Stunned and wide awake now, I asked myself, "What the...? Why am I wide awake and on full alert at this hour?"

And the answer came, special delivery, with great clarity:

> **"Julie, your time on this earthly plane is limited. What are you doing with the time you have? Are you living in alignment with your true purpose and priorities?"**

"Thank you, Universe, for that motivational message," I said inside. Still crackling with electricity, I lay awake, asking myself those important questions. They stayed with me as I rose to see a beautiful Lake Simcoe (Ontario) sunrise.

Then more questions came. And some answers.

Should I be worried? I didn't feel worried. I felt peace. I felt purpose. I felt . . . gratitude.

What would I do with this information? I would live my life in alignment with my purposes and priorities. I would live love.

3

What does alignment look like, for me, here and now? This query is my daily mantra.

Now, nine months after my midsummer "enlightening bolt aha!" I contemplate this week's news of my brain tumor within that earlier message's context: an MRI shows I have brain masses of an unknown type. Being in the space between vague preliminary findings and useful diagnostic or prognostic information is not an easy place to be; it is a motivating one. I am open to learn from this event by being here now, creating meaning and tending my purposes as top priorities.

Today it's time to let my loved ones know about me. I pray that I may do it well.

3

Send Them Love, I Say!

In an email to my sister, I wrote:

I left a message less than two hours ago and my neurosurgeon's assistant just called me back, so that's impressive. He is a "back man," so they sent the referral to their neuro-oncologist, who is a brain operator, and he or his office will follow up. My back surgeon's office took the initiative to call, requesting an urgent follow-up, and found out that today is clinic day in the new doc's office, so I will likely not get a call from them till later in the week.

Just so you know, I will give this one day and then call them. I'm assertive sometimes, and especially now while hanging in limbo status with the knowledge of the masses in my head.

Are they sentient little beings? Send them love, just in case, please.

Maybe we'll get live video footage if and when he goes inside Julie's brain. So, that is my update.

In Love with LIFE!
Joyfully Jammin' Julie"

4

Saying My Peace: Green Bananas

In an email to my closest family circle, each of whom I had informed via phone of my brain findings over the weekend, I wrote:

Today I went to my GP and got a sinus ENT (ear, nose and throat) consultation request going, so I can take care of that part of my issues, hopefully.

My GP will also now be checking with the neurosurgeon to make sure I'm not at risk of seizures (read here: driving would be a bad idea, if so). She also let it slip that the mass (she didn't "think" -- that was her word -- there is more than one) is near my right eye, and that is why they were concerned about visual changes. She has no idea if surgery or no surgery will be recommended. She's not able to guess that.

The MRI report had lots of paragraphs and more than one page and I was not able to knock her unconscious or detract her sufficiently to take cell phone pictures. Since this doctor, who is my usual GP, did not order the MRI scan, she said she was not at liberty to give me a copy. Strange, eh? The same was true of the substitute GP who first told me about this brain issue on the report.

Thursday I will see the endocrinologist memory specialist, Dr. L, who ordered the MRI while investigating my self-reported vocabulary deficits, and unexpectedly found my tumor, and she will tell all. I am a wordsmith, a lifelong educator and writer, and I noticed I was having a hard time recalling some simple vocabulary words when I needed to use them. Dr.

L promised me in an earlier visit that she will always answer all questions about any of my test results or her medical advice.

Meanwhile, I wait for the neurosurgeon's office to call me with an appointment. I did harass, sweetly yet assertively, his assistant's voicemail this morning and left a weird enough message that they'll surely be worried about my condition and speed up this waiting process . . . hopefully. I sounded as grateful, impatient, pathetic and deranged as I could pack into one unified and short voicemail. There are no live receptionists, only call-backs at these clinics. So tidy and unfair . . .

Th-th-th-that's all I know and don't know.

I shall continue to buy green bananas.

5

Doin' the Limbo

The next day's email to my support circle had more detail. I wrote:

Today I saw an ENT (Ear, Nose and Throat) specialist who has me on a new regimen to treat my ongoing sinus issues. He has a copy of my MRI report and said the symptoms I am experiencing sinus-wise are not influenced by (yes, he let it slip, specifically) "the meningioma behind my right eye, a benign brain tumor that many are born with and often live with their entire lives."

The exception is when such a mass is too large or located in a place that it can cause an issue, and then they will sometimes take it out surgically. That step, should it be merited, will be up to the neurosurgeon whom I will see soon.

The neurosurgeon's office did call this morning to say that I will be hearing from them as soon as they have a cancellation. They expect to have one sooner than the next available appointment time (June, three months from now) and will call me to come in as soon as they have a slot open, because they want to see me ASAP. They said cancellations happen every week. So, I sit tight.

I also await the advice on whether I am at risk for seizures and thus shouldn't drive. I want to be responsible for myself in the interim, so Earl is providing me rides when needed. Thank you, Earl.

I have no other news, other than to say I am feeling the stress of this limbo status, and I am tired of the pressure, sinus or otherwise, in my head, face and orbit (eye socket). Thank you for your support, for your healing thoughts, prayers and good humor (please keep 'em coming) and for those highly creative suggestions some of you have made.

Love to you all,
Julie

6

The Strain of My Brain Falls Mainly in This Plane

Life inches forward. In some ways my situation moves at a snail's pace, combat crawling toward who-knows-what-next diagnostic and prognostic outcomes. In other respects, it hurls out of control at breakneck speeds along a roller coaster trajectory. I don't seem to be able to focus on work tasks, chores, simple choices, life goals, what's for supper tonight, etc.

Amidst all, my head throbs and I wonder: How much is sinus pressure? How much is . . . you know . . . the other pressure, the "Mass Who Shall Not Be Named" lurking behind my right eye? Those among you who've had such moments in Purgatory know this feeling intimately. I hope the rest of you never have to experience it.

The truth is that today Little Miss Mass was given her proper name: *meningioma*. No, it's not a family name (unless you count that my sister-in-law had one); it's a type of benign tumor that many people, especially women, are born having. Most are ignored happily throughout a lifetime, but mine has now chosen to be discovered and, eventually, famous. Am I in her service on that trajectory? It seems so.

How was this secret name revealed to me, you might ask? And I long to tell you, so here goes. In my attempt to rid myself of all possible sinus symptoms, I saw an Ear, Nose and Throat specialist this morning, bright and early at 8 a.m. He let it slip, quite generously, during his quick visit that the "meningioma behind my right eye was not influencing my sinuses in the least."

Bah humbug, I say. Anything living within that close proximity might have all sorts of influence. Why, my sinuses and my benign tumor are practically bedfellows and are at least very close neighbors. I would even call them roommates in this hallowed headspace they call home. I did not share these musings with the ENT doctor.

He asked me a few questions about snoring and surgeries, medications and my foreign accent. I answered dutifully, in full Oklahoma twang, pausing for a moment to ask silently if Ms. Mass (she prefers this to Little Miss Mass) had anything to add.

Nothing, came the answer. *Nothing at all.* She's keeping us all in suspense so far.

Returning home with extravagantly expensive designer drugs from the compounding pharmacy, I discovered that the neurosurgeon's assistant had called to assure us that I would soon receive THE call, but this was not IT. Only when someone cancels their appointment will I be called to His Wholiness the Poop's office to have an audience. Just kidding about his name and title. He's Dr. K, Neurosurgeon.

Till I see him, I'll be here, practicing my lines, just as Eliza Doolittle, or any fair-lady- in-waiting: "The strain in my brain falls mainly in this plane."

This too shall pass.

7

"Ab" Is the New Normal

In the next email, I wrote:

Hi, gang. It's been a big day for my brain and me. (Earl's brain too.)

I have an appointment time now on Tuesday morning to see the neurosurgeon mentioned to you earlier, Dr. K. They got a cancellation and will work me in so quickly.

Today I saw the doctor who ordered my MRI scan. Why did she do that, you may ask? I had noticed slight memory issues, lack of immediate recall of common words at times (very unlike me; I make my living as a wordsmith, writing, editing and educating).

She went over the MRI report from the interpreting radiologist, word for word, explaining everything she could. The one item that is worth noting is the slow growing and benign (noncancerous) meningioma that measures roughly 3x3x3cm, or 1.5 inches in diameter, as it is pushing on and abutting my optic nerve center (adjacent to the pituitary gland). The mass is on the outside of my brain, at the base of my skull, not inside the brain itself, but is causing "mass effect" and that means some important stuff (the nerve to my right eye) is being pushed and squished. She is fairly certain the surgeon will recommend removal. There is no swelling evident even though there is squish/pressure.

In her opinion it might be possible to do this surgery through the hard palette of my mouth. Such a surgery has a typical hospital stay of 3-4 days. There is no hair loss if this is the route of access.

The doctor was fairly certain that another MRI study will be done with the appropriate contrast dye. This first MRI detected a bit of movement, decreasing the clarity, and she knows from experience the surgeon will make his own measurements with his own scan(s).

The other MRI findings are probably of no consequence. Who knew such things could hide in brains and not be of concern? Apparently slight anomalies and variations are common stuff, including more tiny meningiomas that aren't of concern position-wise. My circulation to the brain is good. My "hippocampotami" (winky wink) are normal, and even look younger than the usual hippos for my age group.

She will send me her highest recommendation for another neurosurgeon (second opinion) after she does some further credential and doctor-doctor research to find who is best to specifically address my issue. Her recommendation may be the same as my Tuesday neurosurgeon; we shall see.

That's all. I am hanging in here, ready to find out what I must and get on with the next steps so that life can return to the abnormal ways I prefer to live. ;)

Love,
MaMe/Julie

8

Meeting the Beast

Time to meet the beastly good brain surgeon. Preparing for the trip to the hospital I thought, *I am coming to you! Be gentle with me and I will be "patient" with you. En route, I will sit by the sign that says "KEEP ARM IN" and think of my dad.*

My late father's name is Armin. In the book entitled *Daddy, this is it. Being-with My Dying Dad* I wrote briefly about the day I saw the sign KEEP ARM IN on a street car in Toronto and embraced that message to keep him in my mind and heart. Today, on my trip to the neurosurgery consultation, I sat next to the KEEP ARM IN sign, thinking of my dad and missing his verbal support through my brain's ordeal.

My stepdaughter came to support me and take notes during my neurosurgery visit, while I gave full focus to the doctors who reviewed my MRI results and formulated the plan for what's next. The first gentleman I saw was Dr. G, whose name sounds a lot like "gonad"; while the second one was Dr. K, whose name almost sounds like "condom." What are the chances I would get this pair (yes, pun intended)? I am not making this up. The Universe has a seventh grader's sense of humor. And so do I, apparently.

The esteemed neuro team confirmed the likelihood that my little brain squatter is a benign meningioma, may have been with me for many years and may not need to be surgically removed. There will soon be more ways of confirming, including a dye- contrast MRI and visual field testing, since the little meningio-worm (it looks like a curled-up grub or very small human fetus on the MRI cross-section) is pushing my right optic nerve.

They will follow me periodically with these same tests to see if the tumor is stable, growing slowly or growing quickly, all of which are possibilities.

The MRI images show the mass's shape (described above) and the unfortunate fact that my carotid artery runs right through it, thus giving an eyeball appearance to the cross-section view of the curled fetal brain worm. The pair-au-doctors (henceforth conjoined in my sense of humor) explained that in the unlikely case surgery should be merited, the procedure would take place through the side of my cranium and not through the nose or hard palate of the mouth.

She Who Shall Not Be Named (my daughter does not want me to name the meningioma and "get attached" to her) will likely be with me for a long time to come, conceivably forever. Acceptance, to a greater degree than yesterday or the day before, is now in order.

I resolve to do this headache thing better than I am now. Fortunately, with each next person I tell, new ideas of pain management and alternative therapies are being offered to me. I am open to all of them.

At this point I am not disclosing to my wider world that I've an interloper hitching a ride with me wherever I roam, pushing aside my brain junk to make room for hers, and causing me to mindfully wonder: *Am I my tumor's keeper?*

*   *   *

It occurred to me while in this discovery process that my little tumor friend is relatively new. I had an MRI scan of my brain in 1998 when a severe positional headache appeared out of nowhere. There were no tumors found back then, just a socked-in sinus infection deep in my head that caused the "2 x 4 up against the head" pain whenever I lowered my head below my waist, which I did in order to tie my running shoes. Hmmm. . . Seventeen years is a lot of time for a meningioma to develop.

9

When Every Movie Is About Us

Sitting with my brain tumor in the current limbo between medical tests and doctor appointments has been less inspiring to my keyboard than the adventure of "first findings." There hasn't been all that much to write about: headache, less headache, no headache (hurray for those days!); focus, less focus, no focus (those days drain me). I am kind to myself in every way possible. I rest. I meditate. I listen to inspirational voices and musical tones. I do crossword puzzles. I connect with my wonderfully supportive peeps. I drink health-giving potions and let food be my medicine. I cuddle up next to my husband, enjoying his warmth and humor.

When my head throbbing is not too intense to bear it, he and I enjoy watching light, happy and sometimes romantically sappy movies in the evenings or on weekends. Lately, I notice every one of the movie themes mirrors our situation. Or maybe I'm just projecting (pun intended) that similarity. Second-go-round singles meet in unlikely ways, fall in like and in love, meet hurdles and challenges creatively and comically, and some live happily ever after, eventually.

Without deep investigation into the plot of each movie, my beloved and I ask ourselves, "Have we watched this one before?" "Does it look like a fun one?" And then we hold hands and dive in. Usually, this is a pretty good tactic, especially if we select our favorite actors, or at least recognizable ones. We're not watching the Oscar winners; those are not found in this *chick flick* category, as it is most commonly called.

Just lately, I'm surprised to note that our selected movies involve the selfsame issues we are considering (or perhaps we're prompted to consider them because of these movies): tumors, premature death of a spouse, last wishes, messages and gifts discovered after death, end-of-life celebrations, burial options, life and love after loss, etc. We are emotionally riveted as the themes unfold, compelled to know how each one resolves. Premature channel changing, a.k.a. *ChickFlick InterruptUs* , would not allow us to cycle through to acceptance, hope, eternal love and the return of joy.

Sure, we could choose other movie themes. "Everything is choice" is a favorite and well-used refrain in our lives. We could watch animal nature programs or reruns of *Friends* and *Seinfeld*, keeping a safe distance from the Human Nature shows that keep queuing up for us. But I think we'd be missing an important opportunity to vicariously explore the range of life-love-loss long before any such issues present themselves to us. We can plan to plan to plan. And my tumor prompts me to do that.

My beloved husband and I are alive and well. Despite the knowledge there is an alien entity in my head, the present day is full of possibility, love, joy and hope. Our life is a romantic and inspirational love story, and sometimes a rip-roaring comedy.

We're here, healthy, hopeful and writing our own script. And this one's about us. Our love.

10

The Lightening-Lightning of Master Lee

"Go see Master Lee! Do not delay!"

After receiving this sharp directive via a spiritually guided contact of my caring human friend, I promptly made my first appointment with the local Chinese medicine healer, Master Lee. Yesterday was the day we met.

Opening the door to his modest office, the smell of burning herbs wafted toward us in a great wave, piquing my curiosity and that of my husband companion. We waited for a brief time and wondered aloud what my experience would entail. In our wildest dreams we couldn't have imagined the reality of it.

Master Lee seated me near his desk and in broken English asked why I had come to see him. I told him about my brain tumor, most likely benign, pushing things around in there and encircling my carotid artery, and that more tests are pending.

Meanwhile, I received a message to come see him right away, and I told him the name of the one who delivered this spirited directive. He smiled and nodded knowingly.

He took my hands in his, feeling my pulses, and then asked me to lie face-up on his table. He removed the sock of my right foot and found my acupressure points, pressing each with a painful twang. Next he inserted acupuncture needles into my foot, into each of my hands and, lastly, into the outside of my right cheekbone. He connected the ones in my hands and foot to a mild electrical current, dialing it up until I barely felt its *zing*! After setting a timer, he went to sit next to my husband while I took a brief *zap nap*, perhaps four minutes in duration. The timer went off, and he removed each needle.

What happened next I will do my best to describe. Master Lee told me he was going to balance my energy and restore it. I nodded eagerly, as this was why I came to see him; was it not?

With my hands resting lightly on my stomach, I watched his hands moving above me. He rubbed his palms together and twisted an invisible thread with his fingers, reaching up and down from my core. He spun up and down and, as he did so, a powerful sensation grew in each of my hands, a vibration so strong it was audible, not just to and through me, but also to my beloved across the room. The current was unique, not like electric shock, but rather a buzzing energetic force moving into me, through each hand. This occurred without Master Lee touching me at all; the vibration I felt was from the beaming pulse of energy he directed into me.

Coaching me to "release all negative thoughts and fears, 100%," he lightly touched my neck and shoulders, ironing out the tension with his hands. I shook with release as he gently and swiftly pulled out kinks and blocks there.

He was incredibly efficient and I enjoyed each sensation of this powerful lightening- lightning in my body. Master Lee commented to me, "You are so funny," more than once, because I couldn't help but giggle and smile periodically. This was quite a fun adventure and I let myself enjoy it!

Lastly, he moved to my head and touched me right between the eyes. My headache intensified sharply, very briefly. With eyes closed, I saw a light show of colors and shapes. I felt and heard the infusion of buzzing energy, then its release and a cool breezy feeling. The pain was gone.

Without any discussion of what had transpired, he left me to relax while he looked up something on his computer. Finding the translation he sought, he noted it by hand, then showed me the word "asparagus" written on a piece of paper. Master Lee explained to me how to make a blender puree after cooking the organically grown variety, and take it as one would medicine, twice daily. Likewise, I should eat cooked and peeled tomato, one at lunch and supper. After the medical doctors complete my tests and I know what the tumor really is, I should come see him again.

And that was that. He smiled and shook my hand. I paid his modest fee and left his office dumbfounded, buzzing, and profoundly grateful. I felt relief between my temples and throughout my body. I excitedly and tearfully explained my experience to my husband, noting the lack of head pain. Joy, relief and wondrous vibration were my new feelings, and I was without symptoms for almost an hour.

I had new hope in this energetic infusion. That hope is lasting.

I am thankful for my friend who cared for me enough to ask her teacher and, through that conversation, direct me to this magical medicine man.

This was an energetic experience to remember. Wow. And I have a witness!

11

Wishing for Redemption? Not Yet!

"Julia, get to your redemption faster," the email subject line from my airline points source read. *No, thank you!* was my gut reaction to that prompt. *I'm in no rush for my redemption!* And then I questioned: Why do I recoil from redemption?

I did a little research about the concept of redemption on the Internet, finding multiple nuances of meaning in some online dictionary sources.[3] I decided to explore these a bit to see what may have prompted my initial recoil.

- *Redemption is an act of atoning for a fault or mistake, or the state of being atoned.* This definition doesn't bother me in the least. We're all human, and we all make mistakes. To reestablish integrity with others who are affected by the times we fall short, we atone, admirably. Obviously this meaning does not cause my discomfort. I explore further . . .
- *Redemption is deliverance or rescue.* These are great ideas, just fine with me. No discomfort noted.
- *Redemption is atonement for guilt.* Much like the first definition, atonement is the restoration of integrity when one is at fault. Though "guilt" has a stronger connotation of mal intent than does "fault" or "mistake," it doesn't evoke any disconcerting reactions. I delve deeper . . .
- *Redemption is the repurchase, as of something sold.* This brings up not one iffy feeling. Neither does the next definition.

---

[3] Drawing from all of the following: www.dictionary.com, www.merriam- webster. com, dictionary.cambridge.org, en.oxforddictionaries.com

- *Redemption is paying off, as of a mortgage, bond, or note.* I have no problem with this one. Next?
- *Redemption is recovery by payment, as of something pledged.* Not the slightest gut reaction to this definition. Deeper, I dig . . .
- *Redemption is deliverance from sin through the incarnation, sufferings, and death of Christ.* Well, *there* it is! Sufferings and death? Uncomfortable indeed! I do not embrace the concept of sin nor of thinking anyone died for mine, even Christ. I recoil from the concept of redemption achieved in this manner.

What else may I learn from my reaction? I'll sit with that query; I'm on "tumor time."

12

Do I Want to Be a Bobblehead?

Bobbleheads have big bouncy heads and shriveled bodies, way out of proportion, yet comically pleasing. While my latest source of inspiration comes again from an email offer, I see the wisdom in contemplating the question: Do I want to be one?

Short answer: No.

Longer answer: Hmmm, well, maybe in the comical plastic replica sense, but not in the way of out-of-proportion attention to my head, my tumor and my current health purgatory. In other words, I do not want to become *Brain Tumor Bobblehead Julie.*

I've selectively circled my wagons of supportive friends and family, feeling the wisdom of having each aware as She-Who-Shall-Not-Be-Named and I continue on our journey through the unknown and the unknowable. Some call and some write. They offer many and varied suggestions and supportive information. Most of the communications feel very positive, and compassionate understanding freely flows.

While I appreciate that healthy energy flow, I do feel a bit of the bobbleheadedness I'd like to avoid. I do not want life to revolve around my brain issues, adding to my stress and headachiness, which is intermittently very debilitating, by having to converse about how I'm doing moment by moment. On the one hand, it feels good to update folks, especially when they call out of concern or with some kind offer or encouraging suggestion.

On the other hand, I am not a bobblehead. I am a human being. I have a full range of human feelings and issues, many of which are not related directly to my brain tumor. Fortunately, I also have work to do, and I find my work very motivating and rewarding. I count on and look forward to my earnings. My sanity and professional self-image also connect to the purpose and passion I express through my work. I value my roles in the various projects that I co-create with others.

So, getting back to the other hand, I realize that to care for myself I must take extra measures to limit and genuinely give feedback to disproportionate responses to the selective divulgence of my health situation. Only I can provide these healthy limits and feedback. Only I can create the balance I seek in supportive communications, work productivity, time off, play time, exercise, healthy eating, mindful meditation, closing my eyes to rest them, etc.

Yes, I HAVE a tumor pushing my optic nerve, creating cranial *squish*, but this does not mean I AM the tumor. And if I do not want to achieve bobblehead imbalance in my life, then it's time to assert myself *to my self*.

A wise man, Popeye the Sailor, once said: "I yam what I yam and tha's all what I yam." And he also set limits: "That's all I can stands, cuz I can't stands n'more!"

Okay, nuf said. Time to go eat my spinach.

13

Death with Dignity, Breastfeeding and Too Many Onions

"What the hell kind of chapter title is that?" one might ask. "Has this brain tumor finally gone to your head?"

That would be my educated guess, yes. It has gone to my head (has been there all along) and is sprinkling my dreams with all kinds of weird thoughts. Here are three of last night's episodes.

Death with Dignity!

5 a.m. and I awoke with that resounding phrase at the top of my mind. Well, who likes to wake up to a thought like that? It was unsettling, though not altogether surprising. I do support that we should all have that option when the time comes. When the time comes . . .

Unconditional acceptance of weird dream-thoughts is my preferred modality, especially when I desire more rest. I accept the thoughts and let them float on by, while I drift into new dreams. And I drifted into the next one, eventually.

The baby is hungry! She needs to be fed!

And such a cute little baby she was in this dream. Unlike the previous dream- thought, this theme was enjoyable, though for some reason, instead of getting right down to business and breastfeeding this adorable hungry child, I flitted in and out of dressing rooms, trying on clothes, seeking the perfect outfit and sexy lingerie (for nursing a child? Give me a break!), and without much success. Between outfits, I noticed someone was giving the darling child a bottle. I hoped it was breast milk . . . Acceptance. Next dream?

We have too many onions!

Well, this sounds like an emergency worth contemplating to me! It's true, at this moment in time we do have too many onions, having bought one ten-pound bag of them yesterday while an old bag still held several. Is this my *don't buy green bananas* dream? I awoke, this time for good. I shall make soup. Today. While I still have time.

As for the other themes, I have plenty of conscious thoughts about getting my ducks in a row regarding healthcare proxy assignment, advance medical care directives and such, things I haven't handled. If only I had the motivating desire to start those processes and get them completed. I don't. So my dream gives me prompts.

Breastfeeding? Trying on clothes? Cute babies? These dream themes are born of memories, of cherished days gone by. It's nice to linger in those dreams. Acceptance.

14

The Hand on My Forehead

Last night as I slept, a large hand touched my forehead. I felt each finger and even "saw" it so clearly, never opening my eyes. Gratitude and peace flowed freely.

I asked my husband this morning, did he touch my head? No, he didn't do that. He remembers bumping me with a pillow, and I remember that too.

I continue with my daily mantra: *Dissolve with LOVE.* This I say to myself often, letting the words soak in, again and again, feeling so very thankful for all the love and support that surrounds me.

Most of the day I felt energized, productive, alert and capable. Then the headache took over. And here I am, struggling to write anything while the painful pressure pushes and pounds in all directions, reminding me: I am not alone.

I am never alone. I already knew that. But now I also know I've an anomaly in my head that asserts itself on its own timing, morning, noon or night. Aching. Pushing.

"I'm here, Julie." It's She-Who-Shall-Not-Be-Named.

Oh, yes, I know you are here. And I also felt The Hand this morning. So there!

"Lest you forget me, here's another bad hour of head pain to add to your collection."

Well, bad hours are better than bad days or bad weeks. I've had those too. This too shall pass.

Dissolve with LOVE. Dissolve with LOVE. Dissolve with LOVE.

There were things I wanted to do today. People I wanted to call. I don't feel capable now. My life feels hijacked. I might have chosen not to do some of those things anyway, but this persistent headache takes away that choice and leaves me recoiling from each item on my list. It's not a motivating state. It's. Just. Pain.

- Walking outdoors in the sunshine hurts.
- Talking hurts.
- Listening hurts.
- Moving around hurts.
- Reading hurts.
- Sitting up hurts.
- Lying down hurts.
- Typing this hurts.
- It all hurts.

Come again to me, hand on my forehead. Let gratitude and peace flow freely.

15

Fear of Falling

Just as I started to drift into happy slumber last night, I felt a stinging sensation in my forehead. Yes, "in" my head and not "on" my face. It jolted me into full awake mode. This was a new sensation and not a welcome one.

Great, I thought, *should I now fear going to sleep? Will something terrible happen as I slumber?*

Now, the morning after, I just refuse to believe in that likelihood and allow that train of thought to carry me away on its caboose!

Sleep is my very best buddy, my pathway to peaceful and restful equilibrium when plans and developments, pains and aches, feelings and thoughts, should-haves and could-haves of the day have taken their toll on me. Sleep is my reset button.

*   *   *

I have a worse fear: not falling asleep. Yesterday was the most intense pain I've had yet. At least that I can remember. I have a theory that each worst day supplants the former in my memory of worsts. I tried all my therapeutic meditations, mantras, tricks and potions, and eventually decided that bed was my best bet. Sleep brought me relief, as I had hoped it would after nothing else did.

The first time I awoke in the night I felt no pain. I relished that feeling as I drifted off again into peaceful slumber. The next waking was not pain-free, nor the next, when I arose to greet the day. I now have less pain than yesterday, and that is good.

I do not fear sleep, no matter what inflamed ice pick sensations I'm having. Slumber is my escape from physical discomfort and also from other realities I hesitate to acknowledge: I feel trapped by this health development and by my roller coaster of responses to it. Sometimes I feel hopeless and have thoughts I'm not proud to have.

Months ago, when Brittney Maynard moved to Oregon and took her life to end it on the specific terms she chose to embrace, I wrote a blog post about her. How could I have known The Universe would bring me an opportunity to more deeply and personally examine her motives and her life-limiting dilemma? I feel great compassion for Brittney. I get it, and I wish I didn't.

Brittney's life is different from mine. My two children are young adults. I want to be here, sharing in every pleasure and sorrow I am privileged to witness in our lives. My husband and I are busy creating our own slice of Paradise, day by day by day.

I wonder: *How could I leave this life by choice? I love my life. I love being me.*

16

A Brain Tumor Closet Is
No Place to Live

I do my best to stay positive about my health situation and my chosen responses to it. The last couple of days were really a challenge, but I'm feeling more UP today.

When my husband and I watched and read information on meningiomas, I grew discouraged by the facts and statistics. I previously avoided that learning phase but thought I felt ready to do it, and he also thought it was time. Learning gives me an opportunity to figure out what to ask when I next see the neurosurgeons. Each patient's scenario has widely varying outcomes. Mine is "extra special" because of the tumor's location and the way it encircles my carotid artery.

After watching videos and reading the literature provided by the most advanced centers of meningioma treatment and care, I feel increasingly trapped by this development in my health. It will be an ongoing medical relationship. Any thoughts of moving back to the country of my birth some day now seem unrealistic; being monitored and periodically treated (meningiomas grow back) is how life will be going forward. It also may compromise my longevity and/or quality of life.

There is a good side to our gathering the expert information: it opened up necessary discussions. My priorities feel different to me now, and I want/need/hope/choose to honor that shift. For me, life is not "business as usual." It's a carefully chosen trajectory. What a great life lesson to learn, now!

Sometimes I don't feel "safe and supported," and I realize this is a personal issue, one that challenges me periodically. I'm being mindful of that and not making it mean anything or letting it erode my relationships. This is hard to do and not do.

Prayer and meditation lift me in an outpouring of support from friends and family. When my head feels good enough, I work and enjoy near-normalcy. When it's bad, it's just bad. Anyone with severe headaches, and all the hypersensitivities they produce, knows how life-limiting they can be. I never had to learn this fact before.

As I gradually, selectively, come out of my brain tumor closet, I receive mostly helpful, considerate and welcome responses. I don't let the others scare me too much. I am showered with love and light. I bathe in gratitude.

*   *   *

I had an appointment today and learned the following: My visual field results are almost the same, slightly worse than the previous test in the one most affected area. One-quarter of my right eye's field is partly compromised. The ophthalmologist said it isn't necessarily permanent if the nerve isn't compressed too long or with too much swelling. Still, due to the location of my tumor, "watch and wait till something worse develops" is the most likely course of action. I find out the official plan after my next MRI with dye contrast is complete and the neurosurgery team has my results to review.

*   *   *

Telling our two parents was something I held off doing until I could be with them and gauge their reactions face-to-face. I felt this was important so that I could reassure them about all prospective outcomes of my decision going forward.

We visited Montreal, where Earl's very elderly mom lives, to attend a wedding. This gave me the opportunity to be with her and explain. I didn't rehearse how I would share the announcement with her, but when the time came to talk about it, my words flowed easily and she seemed to accept the news without becoming confused or upset. She took it very well, and ever since has been able to understand the various decisions we shared with her. Whew!

Later the same month, I travelled to my hometown in Oklahoma, where my mother resides. A similarly easy scenario took place. My mother seemed to understand what I wanted to convey and has since expressed many times that she appreciates being kept in the loop. I know if I were in her shoes, and my own daughter had a serious health concern, I would certainly want to be informed and updated frequently.

In both cases, it was important to me to be able to see and hear them, to answer any questions and reassure any worries or concerns they may have. Many years ago my late father told me that it's a gift to be included in the sharing of whatever may be happening to one's child. I felt that both our mothers received this news as a gift, and that affirmed my decision to share with them when and how I did.

17

Contrast Gives Life to My Life

Joy.

Who doesn't want more of it?

These days, as I feel challenged by emotional slumps (and volcanic eruptions), I long for more joyful and carefree times.

At the same time, I know that being joyful and being carefree are not the same state of being, and if I want more joy in my life it's up to me to choose it, no matter how "care-rich" each day may be.

This distinction is not a new one, yet it is important for me to integrate in my attitude and experience of daily life. I want to recognize what beliefs, thoughts and behaviors do not serve me well.

- *Buried alive!* This is what I do, unconsciously, when I let myself feel pressed, weighed down and unfairly burdened by current life circumstances.
- *Escape the pain!* Whether emotional or physical pain manifests in my life, escape is not possible. Escape from me? From my head? Really?
- *Why me?* What did I do to deserve this on top of everything else? Am I not a good person? Sounds like a "pity party" to me.

- *I'm so [#$%&*@<] angry!* Yes, I'm pissed off that little ol' me is being so bothered and afflicted. I want to shout, scream and strike out at someone or some thing. And I say and do things that leave me wondering: *Who am I?*
- *Hide! Run! Don't let them in!* I respond this way when others' prescriptivism and concerned advice to me threatens my (emotionally limited) perceptions.

I could go on with this list, but my point is this: *What's the point?*

Centering in my Most Mindful Self, I choose to draw some Lessons to Live By. For these I reflect on Joy and Suffering.

Joy lives deep down as an aliveness that can be tapped throughout all my human experience. It's not contingent on life circumstances or on my surprisingly uninhibited responses to them.

Joy is the cosmic soup of love. It is the strongest emotion in the universe, strong enough to embrace times of delight, frustration, sadness, loss, anger and despair. Joy holds me in the "soul space" to feel and experience everything life has to offer and to come through, spiritually unscathed.

Sometimes suffering arises when I experience great depth through the full range of my emotions and circumstances. This pain is a manifestation of my willingness to live life vulnerably raw and exposed, unprotected and unguarded. Suffering draws my full attention to each moment of life.

Suffering is part of life, inevitable and also powerful: it provides the contrast that illuminates joy. It can spark endurance, character, hope and courage. It moves me past my comfort zones into the realm of heroic possibility and growth.

Suffering is an opportunity to feel compassion for others and myself. And when I suffer, I can reach out in an offer of heart-to-heart sharing and caring.

When is suffering a gift in my life? When I choose to accept it, step into it fully, let my feelings flow freely, all the darkness and the light, without discrimination or attempts to hide from and fear myself.

So, I ask my Most Mindful Self, "How do I grow my joy?" She's quick to answer:

Embrace All That Is.
Welcome All That Comes.

And she adds, most emphatically,

Contrast gives life to life!

18

Calling All Angels

Excerpting from my email to my Let-Them-In group:

Hi, all. Thank you for your ongoing support. I promised you an update and it's taken a great while to be at a point to be ready to share, because the discovery information keeps pouring in. Today was an important milestone along the way, so I'll catch up with what I know.

Today's consultations with the "second opinion" neurosurgery team, including a neuro-ophthalmologist, were rather mind-blowing. The bottom line is my right optic nerve is already adversely affected, though barely so right now. That will be the key factor being monitored in the weeks and months ahead, along with the size and growth of the tumor.

The tumor, though apparently stable in size, is very close to, wrapping around and pushing on some major stuff: right optic nerve, blood vessels carrying vital blood supply to the brain, optic chiasm (both optic nerves cross there), and the temporal lobe of the brain. It's already "too big" (2.5cm is a threshold for taking action, normally, and mine is 3.3cm). The pressure it exerts and the fact it sits there are at issue, as there is increasing risk over time of it causing a wide assortment of effects to all those parts, including blindness, strokes, hormonal abnormalities, memory loss, loss of thermoregulation, and on and on.

It is likely it will need to be surgically removed at some point in time, but how soon is unpredictable. The goals of surgery are to take the pressure off all these major brain components and to determine what exact type of tumor it is. There is no other way to determine its type than to remove some, and they'll remove as much as they safely can.

They do not recommend the "gamma knife" (a one-time concentrated radiological procedure), because of the important vessels and the optic nerve; it's not a choice for this type or location of tumor. Also not very likely would be radiation alone (which, if used, would be spread over seven weeks of daily treatments), though radiation post-surgery could be used to keep the remainders of the tumor (unlikely they could take it all out in this tricky location) from growing back. They do not recommend injecting it with anything because of the vascular involvement (too risky to inject when the blood supply to the brain is so intimately involved, as it appears to be with this tumor) and the location.

The eye/optic nerve specialist said she hadn't lost an eye yet, and she wasn't going to let me, a "blue-eyed Yankee," be her first. She performed her in-office exams and sent me for more precise optic nerve scans at a nearby location.

Today's neurosurgery team has much more experience with this specific type and location of tumor than the one we met with twice previously, neither of whom had ever had one "just like mine" though their more senior partner had. Today's doctors both had experience with my very same type and location of tumor, the senior one being in this skull-based neurosurgical role since 1992. Nonetheless, both teams of neurosurgeons similarly presented the facts that apply in my situation and the choices that are available in the near future. Outcomes can be good, they assure me. Keyword is "can."

This day's ordeal went from approximately 8:00 till 2:00, and I have to go back again soon for a consultation with a radiation oncologist, in addition to some other specialized visual screening. There will be more visits and the next optical monitoring will be around four months with an MRI around six months, barring any adverse development meanwhile.

Post-surgical recovery is generally around six months, though it could be slightly shorter or even much longer, depending on any adverse outcomes.

Those do happen and they resemble the risks of NOT doing surgery: blindness, stroke, loss of memory, coma, etc. Today the most senior member of the surgery team said the words, "Or you could die . . ." We hadn't heard those exact words before. Any brain surgery is risky; this one is especially so for all the reasons why we are now poised to "wait and see" rather than immediately scheduling that event.

I call on all my angels to look after me as I walk the walk ahead.

19

Twists and Turns

For a while we researched how I might have my surgery in a facility with intraoperative MRI technology available. This is not a typical operating room feature. Then we learned that even the best skull-based surgeons don't rely on this tool. Once "inside my head" they know if they have gotten out all that can be excised safely without the use of that technological tool.

I have so much to do to feel that "my ducks are all in a row" before the potentially life-changing step of surgery. I have to have backup for my various *solopreneurial* enterprises, and I'll have to actually TELL people I haven't told so far what's going on. I'm not looking forward to all of it but am making bits of progress in that direction.

Amidst all, I choose to keep the drama to a minimum. Some days that's hard to do.

Assuming I'd have to be shaved on top to "make way for the tumor," I thought of donating my hair. I did a little research and learned the wig-making donation sites won't accept hair with white or grey in it. Those strands don't dye as uniformly as others, so they're not ideal for wigs. *Humph.*

Then I learned my surgery would not require me to be shorn anyway. They simply make an incision behind the hairline for a craniotomy.

*   *   *

With the help of my brother-anaesthesiologist, I connected via Skype with a Minnesota brain surgeon who is considered a leading authority in "my type of meningioma and brain tumor" surgeries. The Q&A session brought me a feeling of reassurance and direction.

While it is his opinion I should have the tumor removed during this calendar year, he does not think I am at so great a risk that surgery is necessary in the next few weeks. So, whew! I have some time to prepare and be sure I've got the best team to operate. The greatest reassurance came from his description of the actual procedure, recovery, risks and benefits.

Leaving the tumor alone will eventually lead to blindness, and I do not want that. So, now I will seek the "right surgical team" to achieve the greatest chance of full functionality as my outcome.

Travelling across the border to have this surgery performed could be a logistical nightmare. I am very hopeful that local Canadian surgeons will be able to accomplish the surgery I seek and with as much skill and experience as those across the border in the U.S. We shall see.

20

To My Daddy in Heaven

Dear Daddy,

It's been a long time since I've written to you. I miss doing that.

We shared so many big and little things in our frequent emails and phone calls. Our conversations shrank the distance and connected us every day. Now that you're gone from this earthly plane, I miss those exchanges dearly. Our subjects covered pretty much everything, because you held a non-judgmental space for me, always.

You once told me that sharing the parts of my life that were hardest to disclose, my personal hurdles and heartaches, was a precious gift to you. When I finally got the courage to speak to you about my heaviest burdens and struggles, you welcomed that disclosure with a safe and accepting embrace. "It's all part of life," you assured me, and you were there for me through each step forward. I do my best to be this kind of nonjudgmental parent to my own children, and I tell them I learned that lesson from you.

When I was a child, we worked in the garden, mowed the lawn and washed the car, side by side. We built and repaired things. As we worked, you sprinkled in plenty of silliness and wisdom. I learned how fun and rewarding it could be to share the tasks that need doing.

As you became elderly and nearly blind, and then learned you had cancer, your example continued to teach me valuable lessons. You met the unanticipated and unsavory tasks, through each new challenge that unfolded, with courage, grace and good humor. When you felt sad or angry, you expressed those emotions too, sharing the full spectrum of your humanity. "It's all part of life," was a centering mantra.

I have some new life burdens now, Daddy. I know that you know what I'm facing. Some days my challenges feel very heavy to bear and the unknowns are downright scary. As I coach myself to open my head to my heart, I feel you with me, helping me carry that load. Now it's my turn to courageously share the bumpy road of my journey and to remember that doing so is a gift to my loved ones.

It was a privilege for me to be with you in the days, weeks and months before you died. Sharing your final moments on Earth was a gift I will forever treasure. You were courageous. Tender. Generous. Honest. Grateful. You inspired me to open my heart and embrace your final chapter as a precious and sacred time.

Wherever I may be on my life's path, whatever obstacles I face, I would like to emulate your example of peace, acceptance and generous love. Thank you for being with me and showing me how. You blessed me then, and you bless me now.

Happy Father's Day, Daddy. I love you.

21

Inner Child to Adult Self, "*Waaaaaa!*

Yesterday I got the more involved eye testing done to determine the extent of changes from the tumor. My visual field's progressively worsening, albeit slowly. Even a year ago, I had changes that an eye doctor didn't mention to me; we now know this after looking at those older tests. Each time I've been tested since, it is a bit worse. Now my macula shows signs of the tumor's pressure, but all of this is still not into the danger zone that would instigate immediate surgery.

Whew! I am not ready.

My attorney friend and I had a chat today about all the documents I need to have in order to make sure my life-and-death wishes are appropriately honored. That was sobering. I had a cry session afterwards, during which my Inner Child whined to my Adult Self, "*I don't wanna have surrrrrrrrgery!*"

My wise husband says it's healthy for me to process such inner conflict. And he may be correct, but I still have the conflict. I don't want to have a brain tumor, nor surgery, nor any of this mess, but it is what it is.

And that's my mantra at the eye of this hurricane: **It is what it is.**

Here's my dialog of Inner Child to Adult Self (and to Anyone Else, for that matter):

IC: "I know you do the best you can. I hope you know I do too. I apologize for my best not being good enough. I apologize for asking too much, more than you have to give."

AS: "I understand. Sometimes. Sometimes I don't."

IC: "Please forgive me for being Brain Tumor Julie, so lame, so often. I never needed to feel safe and loved, just as I am, more than I do now, at this time in my life. I don't expect you to understand, but I wish you did. I try to communicate it. I often fail."

AS: "Please be patient as I find my way. You never asked for this."

IC: "I know."

AS: "Neither did I."

IC and AS, in unison: "It is what it is. And we're doing the best we can."

22

The Illusion of Being in Charge

"I am in charge and I say . . . !"

Her voice rang across the lake this morning, a young mother doing her best to shepherd several young boys kayaking in the water nearby. "Come! Here! Now!"

Oh, how illusive is the concept of control! I smile as I think of it with fond familiarity.

Once, when my own young child ran as fast as her little feet could carry her toward the busy street at the park's edge, I had the hopeful wish that somehow my panicked voice yelling, "STOP!" -- raised to prevent my toddler from the possibility of being struck by a car, could intervene when my own position and ability to run to cut off her trajectory were not enough. I was lucky that day, as my little one decided to veer toward the playground equipment and not into the street at the park's edge.

I did my best to be a good and protective mom. And perhaps I was too protective, as this same child has reminded me at various times while she grew into adulthood.

But hey . . . that *is* the point: she grew into adulthood.

I surely relate to this lake shepherdess's similar desire for her own children.

Now, it is my own greatest desire to know my daughters' children, if they choose to have them. I long to hold them, look into their faces, wipe their drooling chins, chase after them at the park, watch their soccer games and dance recitals, applaud at their school concerts, talk to them about anything and everything, hold them while they sleep, being there, being here, for their sorrows and joys, and for all their parents' (my children's) joyful and sorrowful milestones.

I want to be here to create my own milestones.

Crying out in my deep longing for healthy security, for surety of a future worth living, does nothing to ease the trajectory of the unknown. I know. I've done so, silently, quietly and most loudly, many, many times. I cry and I cry out; it's a release.

I am not in charge, nor am I in control. It would be so much more comforting to live in that illusion, but I can't. Embracing the insecurity of my situation is important to acceptance, to continuing to pursue helpful solutions, to daily sanity.

It is what it is.

And this tumor has its own agenda, lifecycle and yet-to-be-determined outcomes. There is much I can do to discover them, and even to choose their influential bits and pieces, and little I may do to control them.

Okay, I get it. Which leads me to this: How can I be in charge of my reactions?

23

The Worst Day So Far

I thought long and hard about including this chapter. I decided in the end it was an important episode and including it was being true to the full spectrum of my experience.

Imagine screaming at the top of your lungs this next sentence:

*F*CK YOU, G-D!*

This type of talk, let alone screaming out loudly, is not typical for me. Anyone who knows me well can vouch for that. Yet, this expletive sentence is exactly what I yelled; and I stomped and swung my fists into the air, attempting to release the horrible energy I felt rising through me.

My beloved husband Earl was in the next room, and my outcry brought him to tears. No one knew better than he what I was going through in our search for the One True Path forward. I had reached my limit and had nowhere to turn except to the Source of All That Is, to G-d. Headaches, indecision, limitless possibilities and opinions had all taken their toll on me.

Frustration and pain had won . . . for the moment.

As soon as I let it out I felt much better. A weight lifted. I couldn't take back the vitriolic nature of my loudly spewed cry, but I felt assured that the forgiving nature of All That Is could handle well my outburst.

Earl wrapped his arms around me and let me sob it all out. And we both felt better.

This too shall pass, echoed within me as I breathed in new peace and new lightness of being. Henceforth, I looked back on this event as a turning point.

I call it my "F*ck you, G-d day." I've never had another quite like it, but if I do I'll remember how well I survived the first one.

I forgive my circumstances and I forgive me.

24

Frustration Is Often the Name of This Game

Excerpting from emails:

Dr. Z's office is now closed, and they are away, till Monday, August 31. So . . . I can't schedule my follow-up appointment with her, and I'm trying not to cry in frustration right now. Trying is not doing. Let me rephrase: I am not crying, but I am frustrated. Plenty, in fact. Holy !@#$%^&*) (*&^%$#@! guacamole! So there, pthhthththth! And so goes the saga of my brain and me, a never-ending exercise in patience.

In Peace and Tranquility, this life or the next, Julie

*   *   *

Waiting to hear from Boston doctors. My head is hurting lots today. It is what it is. Been wrestling with the devil today, and now I understand what that can mean. I'm doing fairly well physically, dealing with so many pressing "extras" and feeling maximally challenged emotionally. I'm doing my best to handle all the issues and the general stress of having a very poorly positioned brain tumor. I'm bouncing around between tests, doctors, opinions, strategies and now also countries, since I will be going to the Mayo Clinic soon for an opinion as well as visiting another Minnesota doctor. Two more Boston specialists may be next. There is no easy answer to this situation.

*   *   *

One week from now I'll be in Oklahoma for a week, during which time I plan to tell my mom and stepmom about my brain. I've held off till now, as they're both quite elderly. Now, I think if I were in their shoes, I'd want to know. I just hate to worry folks (and have them obsess to me about it, you know?) when I haven't known or chosen any definite direction of treatment.

During the first week of September, I will consult with two Minnesota specialists, including one at the Mayo Clinic. From there I will go to Boston, where two more Harvard Medical School specialists have consented to see me. Unfortunately (or fortunately, depending on the outcome), I am a very interesting case to these esteemed doctors, all of whom have unique experiences, approaches and recommendations of treating my tumor (or leaving it alone, as it is a very risky surgery). I'm young enough that I'm leaning toward rolling the dice on the surgery, but the potential risks are a bit daunting.

*   *   *

We've seen two surgeons in two days here in Minnesota, each with distinct approaches to doing surgery on this type and location (skull-base) of benign meningioma. We have two more to see in Boston, and then we'll decide about going forward with the surgery: when, who (this determines method also) and where, presumably. I haven't anything much to report other than the fact we've made progress and it's good to be moving toward a solution.

Sadly, the relief of headaches is neither guaranteed nor necessarily likely after surgery. About 5% of the time, they're worse. I don't like that news. Likewise, blindness is one of the undesirable risks, but without the surgery it is likely assured over time, as are other unsavory developments. Whatever part of my vision I lose prior to the surgery will not be retrievable, as a rule; so, sooner rather than later makes sense, if I'm willing to risk the procedure at all.

Having Earl, my beloved, at my side, and to ask his own questions, has been wonderfully supportive. I am thankful for his caring presence, just as I am for so many others' on this journey.

Staying here near Minneapolis has its perks: my brother Lou's gourmet cooking, his comfortable home and his own medically informed opinions. He's seen a vast number of neurosurgeries in his role as an anaesthesiologist, and he also can help us review our newly arising questions and concerns.

*   *   *

Yes, I am a Dr. Seuss version of myself these days: *Oh! The Places You'll Go!* HA! That's my life.

One thing all the surgeons keep reminding me is this meningioma discovery is the beginning of a lifelong relationship with the tumor and with the folks who'll monitor and manage my care going forward. They never consider it "over and done with" due to the way many grow back and others can't be fully removed in the first place. It's not a fun prospect, but I'm doing my best to be accepting.

*   *   *

On Wednesday we go to Boston for the final two US doctor opinions we're gathering. Then I see the two Toronto ones again in October. Presumably, after that, we'll be ready to make a decision and schedule surgery, unless we already have decided prior to those; we'll see. I'm confident we'll be on track by then.

I've a headache today, but not the worst sort. Functioning between throbs.

25

Questions for the Doctors

In anticipation of seeing two Boston neurosurgeons, we gathered our many questions. Two previous early September surgery consultations, one in the Minneapolis area and one in Rochester at the Mayo Clinic, were very informative as we composed them.

- Within what timespan should we do the surgery? Or is it necessary?
- How long has this tumor been there?
- What are the percentage risks and outcomes if we leave it alone?
- What are the percentage risks and outcomes if we do the operation?
- What is the length of hospital stay? What is the overall recovery time?
- What complaints do patients have after the surgery?
- How many people get worse headaches after surgery?
- Do you remove the skull portion where the tumor arose? Why or why not?
- Do you retract the brain to gain access to the tumor? Why or why not, and what are the risks of doing that?
- How long does the operation take?
- Who does the actual surgical work? Are others involved and to what extent?
- Do I come back for a recheck after being released from the hospital?
- How do you decide whether to leave some tumor behind or not?
- If it is not all successfully removed, what do you recommend as further treatment?
- What are the chances of it growing back? How fast will it grow back and is there a way of slowing down the regrowth?
- Are stitches removed here at this hospital or do they dissolve?

- Can I be followed at home or will it be necessary to return over time?
- How many surgeries just like mine do you do each year?
- How many total have you done in your career?
- What kind of pretesting do you do immediately before the surgery?

26

Email Trails Through the Forest

Drawing from emails:

The first doc we saw yesterday at Brigham & Women's Hospital in Boston told me about the possibility of *schwannomas,* as they are often also associated with the incidence of meningioma. He doesn't think I have them, though. No sign of them on MRI. *Whew.*

The two doctor visits both went well. We were seen roughly two hours later than my scheduled time of 10:15, and that first appointment lasted till almost 3PM. Really! Then, we had one heck of a fast and furious ride getting to the second one, arriving around 4PM for the 2:30 appointment. No worries on their end, thankfully, because they had a late running, full clinic day.

The doctor we saw at B&W, was first recommended to us by a local Toronto surgeon we saw in late July. One of the Minnesota docs called him "the one who wrote the book on skull-base surgery," saying that all the specialists with that sub-focus in neurosurgery know him, whether or not he knows who they are. We liked him a lot and learned from him. He believes I am symptomatic enough to get this done in a reasonable time frame, but there's no mad hurry. His proposed procedure was most like the Toronto doctor who started to follow me in May. I wonder if all the "older" doctors (which both of these are) prefer to use this method of entering the skull and not having to "touch" the brain, as some of the others do in their procedures. He laughed heartily during our visit, and that's what I really want: someone who gets my lame jokes.

The second Boston doctor, who is on staff at Mass General, was a somewhat younger man who spoke highly of the younger female surgeon whom we saw in late July in Toronto. He has an approach more like the Mayo doctor, who also happened to be younger. He specializes in this particular area of brain tumor removal (there is another person who operates on tumors a little bit further back, another whose specialty is on the top of the skull, etc.). He does not call himself a skull-base surgery specialist, which the earlier doctor did. I don't know where the distinction leaves us at the end of the day, because they both sound like doctors who are almost daily removing tumors like mine or very similar, both in character and in location. Both surgeons talked the right talk and the second doctor also chuckled a bit, though not as heartily as did the first.

Neither Boston doctor gave a "salesy" pitch, though both think getting this thing out soon is a good idea. I have a bit of time, but it's a serious matter to address. We get that. The hospital stays seemed comparable (two to three days) and they want me to stick around for a week or so to get stitches removed (unlike Mayo, who, once they punt me at four days, cuts me loose with dissolvable stitches).

We will likely keep both our local (Toronto) October appointments, one with the doctor who uses the more invasive procedural approach and the other with the less invasive one, to discuss the finer points and timing and to assess where we lean: here in Toronto, or stateside in Minnesota or Boston. Lots to do in the meantime . . .

That's the update!

Thank you for all your support.

*　　*　　*

We saw the one neurosurgeon here on Thursday and I'm still compiling our notes from the questions we asked him. His impression, taken from measurements he made, was that this tumor might have grown some, unlike the radiologists' written reports. The neuro-ophthalmologist also says my visual field test has worsened. The other test she ran on me does

NOT show anything worse, but Earl and I are considering: perhaps sooner is better than later. Surgery is not firmly scheduled, but we'll see what our further appointment brings in nine days.

*   *   *

Hi. It's been a bad headache day today but the weather is inspiringly gorgeous. Fall colors are my medicine.

I told you I was seeing the final doctor today in my "quest for the best." Little did I know she would have still another opinion in mind. So, I will be seeing a radiation oncologist before making any decision, based on today's information.

Surgery may not be the best option, according to this neurosurgeon, who had presented my case to her tumor board so she could gather the opinions of the assembled group with varying subspecialties. I will explain more later when I have the next opinion about the percentage risks of doing either just fractionated radiation (daily weekday treatments for seven weeks, totalling 30) or surgery and radiation, both of which are now on the table again. The Universe doesn't have clarity in mind for me just yet, and I am accepting.

*   *   *

As far as the gamma knife procedure goes, I am not a candidate because of the way this tumor is so intimately involved with the internal carotid and the optic nerve. This doctor (yesterday's) thinks the blood supply to my tumor and to my right optic nerve are one and the same, a very likely possibility based on my CT angiogram and the fact that the tumor hasn't grown but my sight is worsening (an indicator of competition for blood supply). Surgically removing the tumor necessitates cutting off its blood supply (to prevent a brain bleed) and since they cannot tell which tiny vessels supply blood to which (tumor or optic nerve), they might cut off the blood to my optic nerve. She says there is even as much as a 50% chance surgery would have this result).

Anyway, more info will come from the next radiation oncology consultation. I'll update when I know. Don't even have an appointment with him yet. Right now he's out of town and she wants to talk to him to work me in ASAP after he returns, so we're not going through his appointment desk. I wait.

It's looking more likely that to save any eyesight I MAY have to give up one eye's. This is a bummer.

27

Who Has the Time for Time Management?

I started this piece months ago by capturing a title that resonated profoundly. Then and now, it's the same thought that guides me to write on this theme: Time management is an elusive discipline.

Choice by itty-bitty choice, choice by grandiose choice, and everything in between, I manage time. Oh, how I'd love to disown that truth! Really? It's up to me to manage my time? How can I accept that is so and continue to observe myself making choices and non-choices that get me nowhere? Okay, somewhere . . . in fact, right here.

As a surgery date becomes more realistically a definite possibility, I am disturbed, far more than motivated, by my shifting priorities and lack of action taken on them. A better match (than I am manifesting) would be *aligned* priorities and actions.

Here's my time management routine, one rhyme at a time.

I roll over to look at my clock and see
with a blink or two that it's 7:03.
Take time to count blessings and to be grateful.
It's not mine to fight; I accept what is fateful.
I remember the rhyme "Get up outta bed,
(and I say to myself) you ol' sleepy head."

Stretch slowly, breathe out, and then breathe in.
Not breathing at all is a lethal sin.
Make java in jammies; that's how it works.
Self-employment has its several perks.
Sip and delete, delete, delete;
I whittle my emails "down to the meat."
Facebook, Twitter and LinkedIn.
Social media seeds will harvest the win!

As I reach out and make new connections,
my mind is spinning in many directions.
How may I serve your goals today?
"Will you edit my book?" you say?
That's my favorite thing to do!
Of course I'll do it, through and through.
I love to edit, coach authors and write.
Each new publication is outta sight.

The hours rush by; I do each chore.
No matter how much, there's always more.
Today I worked on this and that.
Sometimes I stood and sometimes sat.

Focus is a challenge when my head's in pain.
Sunshine feels much lighter than rain.
I schedule appointments and daily walks.
Make sure to call my peeps for talks.
Friends and family are the very best.
Their care and love help me deal with the rest.

I have a tumor; this much is true.
Yet, I'm determined not to make myself blue.
Some things I may not choose in life.
How I react creates ease or strife.
Staying centered and choosing to release
is how I coach myself toward peace.

Sometimes I'm able and sometimes not.
I accept what is; I get what I've got.

One thought prevails, as I write and vent:
Who has the time for time management?

28

The Secret Sits in the Middle and Knows

"We dance round in a ring and suppose
But the Secret sits in the middle and knows."

- Robert Frost, 1874-1963[4]

The Secret.

We started here in Toronto. The first doctors we saw had never done a procedure on a tumor that was quite like mine; this secret we found out only at the end of our second visit.

We saw more Toronto doctors who had removed tumors just like mine. We listened and learned, took notes and asked questions. We emerged with a clearer understanding than after our first visit with the less experienced team.

We had a Skype consultation with a doctor from the US. Based on what we relayed to him about the Toronto surgeon's approach, the US doctor advised: "Don't let them do that to you." He was commenting on the invasiveness of the surgery, the way the doctor planned to gain access to the base of my skull.

Holy freaking warning, Batman! Surely there was another way to approach this issue.

---

[4] https://www.enotes.com

We saw another Toronto doctor, one with a less invasive approach than the previous. She described what she would do, if indeed she would do it. She planted a brand new seed: "If I were in your position, with this same tumor, I'm not sure I'd have the surgery. It would not be a clear choice." She also suggested that she might go seek other opinions, including from US doctors, if she had that luxury. And I do.

Would you like to dance with me? Whee!

Off to the US we flew, seeing four experts, each with varying nuances of surgical procedural finesse, vast experience and persuasive reasoning. With each consecutive visit we became more convinced: This is the one.

No, this is the one.

No, definitely this one has the best answers. Or maybe that one, because . . .

Because, because, because, because, be c a u s e! Because of the wonderful things he does! We're off to see the surgeons, the wonderful surgeons of . . . Hmmm.

And then we returned to Toronto, seeing each of the two appropriately experienced doctors. We asked. They answered. One has more clarity. One has less. And right now clarity seems unreasonable. There is more that we don't know. So we wait.

We've come full circle, dancing 'round and supposing the Secret will tell. All.

Soon.

29

Current Cannot Be Forced, They Say

"There is no need to force the current," they say.

What do *they* know? I *want* to force the current, or at least to go against it.

I want to paddle upstream so hard that I go back in time.
Back to a time when I didn't know I have a brain tumor.
To a time I didn't have headaches.
A time when my eyesight wasn't slipping away, day by day.
When ignorance was bliss.

Well, fat chance of that ever happening, right? Not in this lifetime.

Perhaps a more constructive stream of thought will be to use the current I'm experiencing as a tool, paddling *with* it in my mind, my heart and my actions. I could take a rest in its momentum from time to time. Fighting the flow leaves me depleted, energetically and spiritually.

Perhaps I can harness the power of acceptance and set some positive intentions for the time that I am grateful to have ahead of me.

This I do believe: Whenever my personal intention aligns with The Universe's intention, I work *with* the current, I am part of something eternal, infinite and good. Alignment helps grow the healthy potential in my life and the lives of those I touch.

Now feels like the right time for some intrapersonal Q&A to refine intention.

Q: How will I act to grow the expression of goodness in my life?
A: I'll experiment and have some fun while thinking big.

Q: Just how big is my big?
A: I will "come out" of my tumor closet and have a public conversation.

Q: How does this intention create goodness?
A: If my story can help others who face similar issues, this is healthy and positive.

Q: What will be my media?
A: Book, blog and YouTube, along with proper public promotion of the same.

Q: So what am I waiting for?
A: I'm ready. Obviously, I've already started writing. Today I'll start the recordings.

This intention feels empowering and has the potential to connect me to others in a way that assists me and possibly assists them.

"Go with the flow," they say. I'll join my paddling with the current of The Universe and get someplace I've never been.

30

Transformational Love and Grief

From an email exchange:

To My Dear Friends,

Three years ago today my father passed away. I was privileged to be in that moment with him, a time I will forever cherish. He lives on in joyous and loving memories, in the light, purpose and peace he kindled in me. Every day I miss his smile, his special style and the way he shared from the heart so generously. He taught me far more than I'll ever consciously know. His legacy of love endures and inspires me.

I am grateful for All That Is.

Feeling so much love for each of you, sending you health and peace, joy and smiles, Julie

*   *   *

After this email above was sent, I received a note of concern from a dear friend, who believed wholeheartedly that prolonged grief for my father had manifested in my body as the tumor in my head. She encouraged me to focus on the celebration of life and joy versus on death and grief. She saw my recovery hinging on this choice of my direction. Below is my response to her.

*   *   *

Thank you for your loving intentions. Please be assured that I celebrate life every day. My grief is integrated very healthily, I believe with my whole heart. It is neither sadness nor negative energy that I experience. On the anniversary of my dad's passing we celebrated with a great sushi dinner and toasted his wonderful life and the many happy memories. I felt so much peace and love.

I know for one who may not have experienced a similar paradigm of *transformation through loss* it could be hard to understand, but embracing death as normal and natural brings life and value to my life. There is no abyss that I face. I experienced another dimension with my father after he died. It was such a beautiful gift. I was left with a new perception of *this* dimension, and it is a perception I can return to by choice.

Collecting, reading and publishing people's stories helps them to feel their own freedom and release, just as the heart-to-heart sharing is what I feel from all those who've expressed their value in reading my book (*Daddy, this is it. Being-with My Dying Dad*) and other writing, or in hearing my interviews. It's so rewarding and uplifting for me to have this role. Literally hundreds have shared with me that I connected them to a new lightness of being, a new aliveness, because they can now embrace *their* grief as a natural part of life after loss, not a place to be stuck, but a fully integrated and healthy part of those who love and have lost someone dear to them. Death is final, but what we do with that fact can transform our lives forever. This is what the healing and bereavement support professionals call *good grief.*

For me, this experience has brought so many wonderful people into my life, so many connections and professional directions that I would never have accessed without publishing my story and then reaching out to others to share it. You see, I send an introduction to my book to support professionals -- social workers, clergy, hospice and palliative caregivers, nurses, doctors, etc. -- all around the world. If they are receptive, I send them a complimentary copy to review, share and place in their lending libraries. It's one small way that I honor my father, and it feels so uplifting to do so. I am told, by so many, that my little story is the best *how-to book for dying* they've ever read.

This is the legacy of which I speak. My dad, through his example of how it can be done, left a gift of life for my family and me, and it has also been a blessing to many other lives. Whether or not we know someone who is dying, we can all learn how to do it better, how to *be-with* someone (and with ourselves) and not to fear the last chapter, but to create it to be a lasting legacy of love and life for our families and our communities. This I believe with my whole heart.

So, I ask you for your acceptance of my path and purposes, my passion around this topic. It is one that sorely needs to be transformed, as our culture generally shuns and devalues the whole arena of death, dying and the end of life. Who among us is going to change that? In my mind, it is up to those who are not driven by their fears and cultural taboos, but are motivated by love and support. I am an educator and a curator of stories. It is my chosen role and I have never been happier than when I am able to be of this service in others' lives.

I hope, if you will reread the email I sent earlier, you will see the spirit of Love and Light with which it was written. It is not a place of sadness to which I return in memory. My father was a healer in life, a Bio-energetic therapist whose gifts were shared with all he knew. He shared them most generously with me, and I feel abundant gratitude for his role in my life. It is an ongoing bond of delight and purpose, of such blissful experience that I feel very blessed to have as a lasting treasure. I call on that joy and that love to heal any areas of my life that are lacking. I have so much gratitude for the bonds that uplift my spirit and show me the way.

With so much love and gratitude for your intentions, my friend, Julie

31

What Isn't and What Is

People my age and older grew up listening to a jingle: "Happiness is the taste of Kent." Kent was a popular brand of cigarettes, one of the first that had a filter. So many years later, as this jingle came to mind, I thought, "Happiness *isn't* getting lung cancer, heart disease or COPD. Happiness *isn't* the after-taste of Kent."

Then I started thinking: sometimes it's easier to identify what something *isn't* rather than what it is. Which led me to: What *isn't* about my situation right now? What *isn't* the case about learning to live with a brain tumor?

It *isn't* a problem that I blame myself or anyone else for having. I'd like more than ever to take responsibility for this tumor; however, they tell me it's not due to anything I may or may not have done. There is no blame to attribute to anyone or anything. Is it a problem I can responsibly manage? The jury is still out on this question.

It *isn't* a situation to which I am overreacting. In fact, I am acting appropriately, pursuing various possible resolutions without drawing premature conclusions. It is a serious situation, but it *isn't* something that has to ruin the rest of my life. It *isn't* innately horrible, and it could be a whole lot worse. Just today my neighbor related that her younger sister recently died of an inoperable brain cancer. I have a benign tumor that may very likely not shorten my life at all. In the time I have left, I may become wiser, stronger and more able to serve others, even if I have permanent or lasting issues. How will I react to having it for the rest of my life? The jury is still out on this one too.

It *isn't* helpful to me to frame it negatively, chastising myself for its effects on my daily life. It is a story I tell myself, mentally composed either as a challenge I am meeting or one that has me beat. I get to choose the plot details, even if I may not choose the big events along the way. It *isn't* more powerful than my own positivity. This verdict is in!

It *isn't* a trap. It's a circumstance with options, some more restrictive and some less so. Nonetheless, multiple paths are available to me. I am not a helpless victim of an all-powerful tumor. I have the ability to manage my reactions and directions. Case closed.

It *isn't* the only focus in my life. I am passionate about many pursuits, personal and professional. I care deeply about the loving choices I make in each of my relationships. I enjoy hobbies, socializing with friends and pursuing creative interests. I am an avid reader and an extemporaneous chef. I enjoy serving my business clients and am proud of the work I do on their behalf. It is hard to imagine the loss of fulfilling any of these various life foci. Still, I know if I lose my ability to do some of the things I enjoy I will have many other things that make life worth living. And life is well worth living.

It *isn't* what it *isn't*. It is what it is. These are concurrent life sentences. Smile.

32

Indecision Time!

Hi to my loved ones. :) Thank you for all your support.

Yesterday, after seeing the radiation oncologist who heads up the entire Toronto University Health Network brain team (neurosurgery, neurology and brain cancer treatment), I have this takeaway consensus opinion to contemplate.

My case was presented to the tumor board with supporting evidence: CT-angiogram showing blood supply and density of tumor, MRI showing virtually no growth since February and slowly worsening visual field in my right eye. Considering all factors and appearances, the group's opinion is that total removal of the tumor will likely not be possible. It's too tightly bound and growing completely around the internal carotid artery; it is very dense versus fluffy AND may share micro-vascular blood supply with the optic nerve. They think this because it appears to be competing for blood supply, as evidenced by the changing status of my visual field (noted in my own daily observations of fluctuating visual clarity).

To safely remove it, a responsible surgeon would likely leave the critical part of the tumor: the part on the interior side of the carotid, pressing on my optic nerve and hovering over the optic chiasm. This being the case, presumably (they estimate 50% or greater likelihood of above scenario), I would still require radiation in order to stem the tumor's future growth, which if left alone would cause blindness first in one and eventually in both eyes (it actually would occur partly in both eyes before the two go completely, a predictable sequence).

Why, they ask, would I opt for the risky surgery when radiation will be needed afterward anyway, in all likelihood?

Risks of radiation are distinct from those of surgery and are long-term versus short- term and immediate, developing in 5, 10, 15 years or more, in a slightly raised percentage versus the rest of the (aging) population:

a. Development of brain cancer or other tumor growth/regrowth
b. Memory issues
c. Cognitive issues in higher/executive brain function
d. Stroke (which can be ameliorated with lifestyle changes I'm already adopting)

With surgery, I risk having stroke, blindness, death, other eye issues, and a few other less risky things, but these are significant considerations: 5% chance of one or more under the best of circumstances, and with the likelihood of shared blood supply (tumor and optic nerve) the risk of right eye blindness is even greater than the original estimate of 5%.

That's pretty much it in a nutshell. I'm struggling with a persistent headache right now. Not rushing into any decision. At least not today.

Love to each of you, Ma Me / Julie

*   *   *

Hi there. Thank you for your permission to vent. It's so important to have that outlet and you are such a sane one, not taking it personally or "prescribing" anything that adds more stress to my course of action and decision making.

Our plan is to get a list together and ask all the neurosurgeons and the radiation oncologist, the neuro-ophthalmologist and also the memory doctor. My GP doctor friend here in Canada just gave me some more good questions to ask.

I'm going to rake leaves now after having done lots of discouraging Google research about radiation, surgery and so forth. The way we see the array of choices is this:

a. Surgery followed by radiation, if needed
b. Radiation alone
c. Do nothing, decisively
d. Wait some more and choose one of the above when the time seems right

Have a great day.

Love,
Julie

*   *   *

One of my doctor friends wrote that she wondered what the risks would be (from the radiation) to the surrounding tissues, such as the optic chiasm and optic nerve. She also wondered if the radiation caused the tissue of the tumor to necrose and reabsorb. That made me begin to wonder: Would there be side effects of the swelling, necrotic tissue and blood in that area of the brain? What would be the conceivable short- and long-term side effects of that stuff? How long would I have to wait until the tumor shrinks and the effects of the acute radiation are resolved?

Another doctor friend reminded me to find out how successful radiation would be. I had noted the side effects of radiation but not how effectively the radiation oncologists think they can treat the tumors. He also prompted me to find out if radiation might make subsequent surgery difficult or impossible. I realized I ought to ask about that, as it might eliminate the option if surgery was otherwise advisable in the future.

I thanked my two friends for these considerations. Reviewing all the information we'd been given, this is what I learned: the success rate of fractionated radiation alone is 85 - 90%, and getting better with each passing year, so if they take out the old data it's even more successful at stopping tumor growth.

Since no one mentioned subsequent surgery and any difficulties that may present after radiation, I resolved to pose that question to the radiation experts.

*   *   *

[The following was sent to the surgeon and the neuro-ophthalmologist with whom I had previously consulted.]

On Saturday, I had an MRI.

Previously you had sent me to visit with Dr. C, and last week I saw Dr. L [both neuro- oncologists]. After examination of my CT-angiogram, showing blood supply and density of the tumor, the MRIs showing virtually no growth since February, and the slowly worsening visual field in my right eye, Dr. L's opinion is that total removal of the tumor will likely not be possible. It's too tightly bound and growing completely around the carotid with no visible space or "seam." He also held the opinion that it is very dense AND may share microvasculature with the optic nerve. He suspects this because it appears to be competing for blood supply, as evidenced by the changing status of my visual field (some days better than others), while the tumor hasn't grown in size appreciably.

Dr. L says, to safely remove the bulk of it, a surgeon will likely leave the critical part of the tumor: the portion on the interior side of the carotid, pressing on my optic nerve and hovering over the optic chiasm. If this is the case, and he estimated to me a 50% or greater likelihood of this scenario, I will require subsequent radiation in order to stem the tumor's future growth.

He asked me: Why would I opt for the risks of surgery when radiation will be needed afterward anyway, in all likelihood? He indicated there was no advantage from his point of view of de-bulking the tumor; he will use the same amount of radiation either way, a level determined by the optic nerve versus by this size tumor.

Now I am confused and reconsidering my options. I value your opinions on this matter. And I have these questions:

- If the odds are that I'll need radiation anyway, down the road or even in the short-term, do you still recommend surgery over fractionated radiation as a first step? If so, why, specifically?
- If I choose to do fractionated radiation as a stand-alone treatment, would you be able to do surgery later if the tumor is growing or causing me issues?
- Are there factors that you believe weigh heavily in favor of surgery versus radiation?

I ask you for any information that can assist me in making this very difficult decision. What is your assessment of the latest MRI? Thank you for your excellent care and attention. Your timely response will be appreciated.

Julie

*   *   *

The nurse practitioner with the neurosurgery department responded to let me know they would be reviewing my case at their next Tumor Board, where they have all the specialists around the table. She said they would be in touch soon after that meeting.

*   *   *

The Mayo Clinic doctor responded to me too and it was not reassuring regarding me having radiation alone. His biggest concern was that I will likely develop visual deterioration if I leave my tumor sitting as it does on my optic nerve. He reiterated that surgery would remove the tunnel surrounding the optic nerve, thus allowing it room to swell if I do require radiation after surgery. He also made the point that surgery could make my tumor a potential candidate for a single-session of gamma knife radiation. He strongly advised surgery for my tumor, and if radiation were needed afterwards there would be a 97% chance of tumor control.

I reminded myself: of course a surgeon recommends surgery. It's the tool of his trade and the method he knows best.

*   *   *

A close friend weighed in to remark on the long journey of my discovery and decision. She wondered what will happen if the second tumor board doesn't agree with the first? What would I do with such an outcome? I too wondered the same thing. She advised me to go into silence, for a day or two. If I stop researching and weighing statistics and just let my inner wisdom make the decision based on all of the research I have already done, my body might just tell me what it needs for me to do, so it can begin to heal itself.

I am clearly blessed with such smart friends.

*   *   *

One of my family members reassured me that my hesitation to jump into a solution without checking out all the variables is quite understandable. I'm glad some folks get it.

Folks are praying for my healing, for my decision to be made clear and for me to have peace of mind in that decision.

I feel very well loved and supported and am so grateful for that.

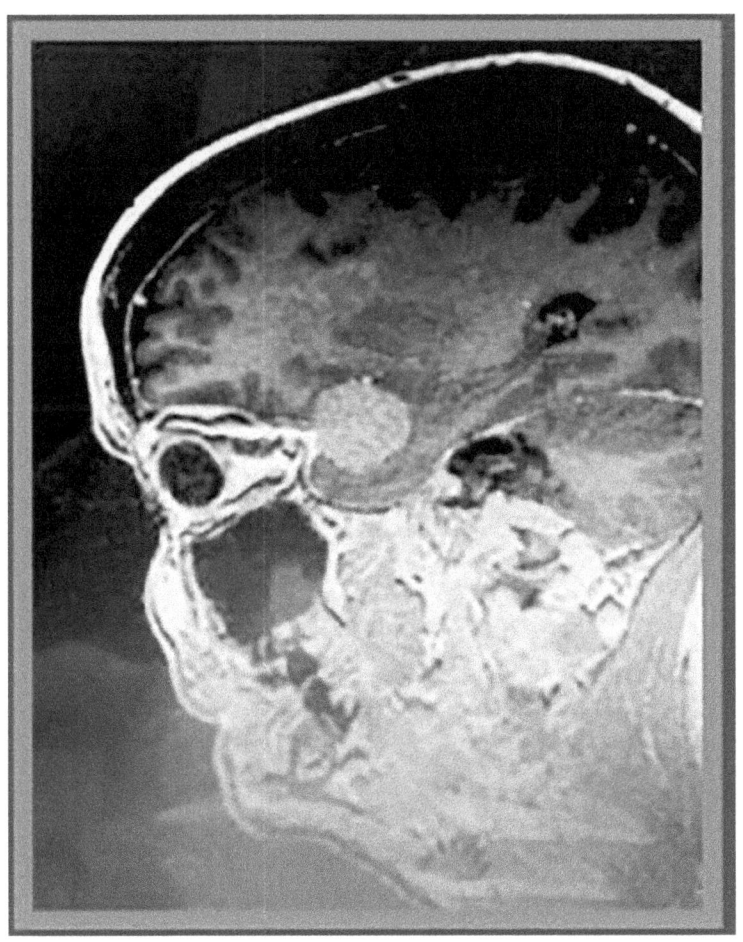

My Tumor in Profile

33

Put Off About Putting Off

Dear Ones,

Now we have another neurosurgery team, from a second hospital, bringing my case to their tumor board this Thursday. Therefore, just a few minutes ago, I put off (indefinitely) the initial appointment with permission signing, fitting for my radiation mask and CT/MRI tumor mapping for the physics of radiation, all of which were scheduled for this Friday the 13th.

Frankly, I am so sick of this whole saga that I'm feeling quite disappointed with myself for not taking the leap and making the commitment. We -- Earl and I -- were not in agreement about proceeding. I deferred to his hesitation. And as time passes, I agree with it more and more. The more we know, the more we'll know. Maybe the two tumor boards will agree, and that will make the next step easier.

It is what it is . . . As my doctor brother Lou so wisely said, "It may be growing slowly, but it is slowly growing." He thinks I should do something soon, one way or another.

Julie

*   *   *

A dear friend responded with so much compassion, reminding me not to be disappointed with myself about anything. She told me to remember this is the time for utmost self-compassion. If I would not be disappointed in a friend or relative who was making similar decisions; if I would be totally understanding, empathetic and supportive; I should give myself the same benefit. Of course, she's correct.

It's time to take myself gently by the hand, and tell myself how well I've navigated this extremely difficult situation. I've been thorough in my research, gone to great lengths to digest a huge amount of very detailed information, and exercised patience and judgment in weighing all the factors. I've tapped emotional reservoirs as I've ridden the roller coaster of it all.

I will be as good to myself as I can be. I deserve it. And I won't be upset if my patience runs thin.

*   *   *

[I emailed Earl, my beloved husband and partner, with the following when he asked me about postponing.]

I don't know of any good reason to do so at this point. I'll send Dr. L my questions today, though I haven't finished my list of them yet.

I'm tired of being a tennis ball in this game of life. Am I being hasty?

It's kind of like giving up against the current. Will I now drown or get across the stream to better times?

*   *   *

[Dr. C, the surgeon, called me, and below I summarize our conversation.]

Dr. C disagrees with the [other] tumor board's opinion. He thinks the tumor can and should be removed before any radiation, which may not ever be needed and certainly not right away, unless the tumor is of a different type (faster growing) than what they suspect now.

My most recent MRI, now nine months' time since the first one was done, shows measurable growth, 3.07 to 3.53cm in one direction and 1.46 to 1.73cm in another, at least according to his preliminary views. The radiologist's report is still pending, so he did his own calculations based on two cross-section views.

To summarize Dr. C's conversation with me, taking out the tumor, surgically:

1) Allows for a definitive tissue diagnosis, so my family and I will know what type it is

2) Decompresses the optic nerve and the brain, both of which do seem to be bothered by the pressure it's exerting

3) Gets rid of bulk, so that IF future radiation is needed, the area being radiated is far less (which results in less scatter to surrounding healthy brain tissue)

And further:

4) He also thinks the little blood vessels coming off the internal carotid are more of a risk than the ones supplying blood to the optic nerve. He said they can be made more brittle with radiation, thus more prone to stroke in future.

5) He thinks there is a "seam" that can be used to pull the tumor off the carotid, hopefully not too overgrown by tumor and blood vessels to do the job that he thinks he can do. He says there is always a seam due to the way the thing grows up and around the carotid from the base of the skull.

6) There is no way to definitively tell about density till he gets in there and accesses the mass, but if he didn't feel confident about the good possibility of removal, safely, he would not recommend it.

7) If he gets inside my head and doesn't think it's safe to do the surgery, he won't proceed.

8) He will discuss my case at his hospital tumor board, either today or next Thursday, to get a group opinion from all in attendance.

9) If the tumor regrows in future even just slightly "off" of the optic nerve and chiasm, gamma knife (a one-time, more concise and less risky) radiation may be used to take care of it.

10) Since my tumor is growing and eyesight worsening, the priority of my surgery gets moved up the list.

11) As pertains to future mutability and regrowth, 10K remaining cells are less worrisome than 10 million.

* * *

Another precious friend weighed in, telling me I'm right about there being such a lot of information. Most people think they have some tough decisions to make in life, but they are usually in a much different league than where I am now, he told me.

More options mean a more complicated decision, even if there are more possibilities. He assured me that my life skills and beliefs will help me make a good choice. Since no one gives a guarantee with any of the options, it is good to know they are all choices of the best surgeons in the world. Ultimately, it is my decision alone to make, and I'll have many prayers and much Light coming my way, and many people will be standing right next to me when I make my decision. I feel totally surrounded by Love and appreciate his words to me.

* * *

And still another friend wrote with supportive words. Again, I am surrounded by love. She was in denial earlier when she read my message. She expressed that she could not imagine my sense of fear, urgency, yet wanting to be decisive for what seems the best. She and her husband were both praying that whatever decision I make ends up being right for me.

* * *

I've so many dear friends sending support and love. Another wrote to ask what was going on. She wondered if I was in a super funk because of all the 'options'. It seemed to her I'd gotten to the point of going with the advice of whomever I believe and trust the most. That may not be the best way to approach a serious medical decision, but it may be my last resort. She thinks I'm an anomaly, and they just have to figure me out!

34

I'm Losing My Fuzz

The MRI report was as follows:

CLINICAL HISTORY: 59-year-old female. Follow-up clinoid meningioma.

TECHNIQUE: Multiplanar multisequence MRI of the brain without and with gadolinium, focused around the area of interest.

COMPARISON: MRI brain August 18, May 19, and February 23.

FINDINGS: Large extra-axial mass in the right parasellar region centered around the right anterior clinoid. This mass has mildly lobulated but well defined margins, and enhances homogeneously postcontrast. It measures approximately 3.4 x 3.1 x 2.9 cm in transverse, anteroposterior, and craniocaudal dimensions, and has slightly increased in size since the MRI from February 2015.

The mass slightly extends into the lateral aspect of the right optic canal with focal compression of the right optic nerve. The chiasmatic right optic nerve and the optic chiasm are displaced medially by the tumor, without evidence for encasement.

Equivocal mildly increased T2 signal within the right optic nerve. The right optic tract is displaced superiorly.

The mass circumferentially encases a short segment of the proximal supraclinoid right internal carotid artery, and nearly circumferentially encases the more distal portion of the supraclinoid right internal carotid artery and the proximal M1 and A1 segments. Slight narrowing of the right ICA lumen as it penetrates the dural ring and enters the tumor, but the more distal right ICA appears to have good caliber.

The cavernous sinuses and the Meckel's cave appear preserved. The right medial temporal lobe is compressed by the mass, without parenchymal signal alteration.

No significant ventricular effacement, midline shift, or hydrocephalus.

IMPRESSION: Large right parasellar extra-axial mass as described above, most likely a meningioma. Mildly increased in size since February 2015. Note is made of small amount of tumor extending into the right optic canal. The mass completely encases a short segment of the supraclinoid right ICA, where there is slight focal luminal caliber reduction. The more distal portion of the right ICA and the proximal M1 and A1 have near circumferential encasement by the tumor. Mass effect on the optic apparatus.

* * *

Dr. C's wrote back to me, once again going over the goals of any possible surgery, which would include tissue diagnosis, de-bulking and decompression of the optic nerve, chiasm and temporal lobe. He made the point that diagnosis is often very important in terms of future management; although mine is most likely a WHO grade 1 meningioma, they cannot be sure it is not grade 2.

Since my recent MRI had not been reported yet, his opinion was that it looks like it has grown a few millimeters. With that growth, he thinks surgery is indicated for the above reasons, and it does not look any more dense than any other meningioma. It is often difficult to be certain, based on the imaging characteristics beforehand, whether the tumor is fibrous or otherwise, although it does look calcified on CT, according to Dr. C. Even in calcified meningiomas, very often they just have micro- calcification and are actually not that firm, although not always.

He told me he thinks the site of origin of my tumor is probably lateral to the carotid. The biggest risk is in the perforators at the carotid ICA bifurcation, and as he told me before, there is still a risk of potentially serious complications such as stroke or loss of vision, more likely related to the small perforators and less likely from injury to a larger vessel.

The bottom line was that he would recommend surgery and that if I needed radiation, it would be as a second treatment option. He would review this with the Tumor Board and see what the group felt.

* * *

Forwarding to me all of the above information, the nurse practitioner added an email note to tell me the tumor board unanimously supported the role of surgery first. She hoped this would help with my difficult decision.

* * *

I wrote to my friend:

Yesterday I was so depressed about all of it. Leaning back toward surgery, though not happy about any of my options. The bugger is growing, last MRI showed. *Sh*t.* I just want to go away, get away, from me . . . I prefer not to think, as thinking makes it all much worse.

Surgery is most likely. I had more doctor calls today to follow up with me. The tumor is growing, and it's into my optic canal. The question is *where, who and when* to do it? Okay, that's three in one. I'm off to go pick up the latest MRI disk now.

I'm very well supported by Earl and others; just have to make the decision myself, ultimately, and they threw some new considerations at me last week, so . . . I feel like a tennis ball rapidly losing my fuzz.

Fuzzy wuzzy wuzn't fuzzy, wuz she? Geez, what I'd give for a carefree week, just one. Hugs and love, my bud,

Julie

* * *

My husband Earl wrote to his three daughters:

9 a.m. Friday. We were originally supposed to meet for [Julie's] mask fitting today to be ready to do the radiation, but we cancelled it on Monday so another could have a spot.

I am shedding tears typing this now after reading the emails that came before, and with hesitation decided to share this email. Sometimes suggestions, ideas, and comments allow us to learn more.

Our contact with you and others over this year has decreased for many reasons pertaining to her tumor. Really Julie's explanation of her tumor is a very small part of what has been happening. Discussing constantly changing strategies, results, planning, options, and upsets all take time.

It's really easier to make a decision when there is no choice, and now we have been given choices, so it's been very difficult. Each doctor talks to us from his/her perspective, and each has differing thoughts, ideas, and ways of approaching this situation. It takes too long for any doctor to tell us the entire story, to know most about our situation, and so we have been doing our best to 'piece meal' the information from seven doctors, their fellows, an eye doctor, and a few radiologists, so far.

One part of this is that we really appreciate having other doctors and many people to talk with us, as their comments, questions, or ideas have us searching for answers; and we have gained in our knowledge. Really, this advice and goodwill have come from friends and family all over North America.

So, I believe, over the next few weeks we will have our decision.

I am writing this, as I believe it's so important to share these issues. And when it's your time to have issues, may I strongly suggest you also share them with others whenever possible. Thirty-six heads are better than two.

11 a.m. We are receiving calls and information and emails from more doctors and support teams, and now have decided that the best direction is to have the operation.

Yesterday the tumor board met with doctors, radiologists, and others and all agreed that having the operation is best versus radiation.

Having this decision to do the operation is finally handled, and I found this to be a relief, as was also hearing yesterday's and today's doctors' positive phone calls. We are able now to cancel a variety of meetings and now concentrate to handle the big issue.

1 p.m. Where will we get this done and which doctor to be selected to complete the operation? This is a very difficult decision, as all three cities--Minneapolis, Boston and Toronto--have both different and good features and benefits. Which will be the fortunate doctor to heal Julie's issue? The choice will be Julie's.

2:30 p.m. Julie just went to the hospital to pick up the MRIs, so they can be sent to the three out-of-town doctors.

Love,
Dad

*   *   *

One surgeon wrote to ask how I was doing. She knew I had met with Dr. L, the radiation oncologist, and she was checking in to make sure all went well, that I was comfortable with my decision, and if there were any questions I might have for her to address.

*   *   *

And I responded to her:

Hi, Dr. Z. It's so very kind of you to follow up. I hope to finalize my direction as soon as possible. Is there any way to see you at your next clinic, if a face-to-face meeting is advisable?

You were correct; this decision has been difficult. As you are aware, we have visited with a variety of surgeons. Your sincerity and generous sharing of knowledge, giving us the time to talk and consider all we were hearing, was very helpful, even while considering radiation. We believe we are in good hands with you and Dr. G.

We met with Dr. L and then I had my MRI scan. This one (results attached) shows measurable growth since the February one, and even since August, since minimal growth was reported then also. It appears to have grown into the optic canal.

With this new information, the tumor board that convened last week reached an about-face consensus: surgery is recommended over radiation. I believe Dr. L was in attendance at that meeting, as were other radiation oncologists, neurosurgeons, and the neuro-ophthalmologist, who has urged me to have the surgery from our first meeting.

With this conclusion, I am ready and now considering where and when to have the surgery, putting radiation aside as a second-line approach, if needed in future.

This leads me to ask:

- How soon could you and Dr. G perform the procedure?
- Do I meet with the both of you prior to surgery, or what steps remain for us to finalize and expedite the process?
- Does your proposed surgical procedure remove the portion of the tumor that is growing into the optic canal?
- Does this development create complications we haven't discussed?

Thank you very kindly for your support and accessibility. Have a nice weekend. Julie

* * *

Dr. Z responded promptly to arrange a meeting in person when we could review all the information and remaining questions. This way we could see how best to strategize.

* * *

A nurse friend weighed in from afar, saying she could not imagine the toll that my search for treatment must be taking on me. She thought it must be scary and that I want to make the "best" choice.

She reminded me of this saying: "Not to decide, is to decide." No treatment will be perfect (medicine is more an art than a science), but whichever treatment I choose, I will be starting on the road to recovery, and improving my situation and prognosis. Just as my brother expressed, her concern is that the tumor continued to grow over the last several months since I found out about it. As it grows, my options - and odds of recovery and complications - are adversely affected. She sincerely hopes that I can find the peace of mind and courage to take the next very important step of making a decision and starting treatment ASAP, for my life's sake.

I know she is coming from a place of concern and love. She wants what's best for me!

*　*　*

My friends lifted me with love in each email or talk that we had. Another said I should go with my gut feeling, but make a decision soon, so I don't lose my sight!

Each one told me I have their love and support. They're there for me.

One said he was glad I have the resources to check with all these people in all those places. He said he was sad to hear that my vision is getting worse but, on the other hand, he could tell me he looks the same as he did twenty-five years ago and I would have no reason to doubt him! Or maybe he could tell me he looks just like Cary Grant in his most famous days . . . He, like all the others, said he knows I will figure out what the best course of action is for me.

*　*　*

Hi, Lou [my anesthesiologist brother].

Right now I'm leaning toward a two-doctor male-female team in Toronto who will do the deed. One started the skull-base neurosurgery program here many years ago. He has forty years of experience. The other has been doing it for ten years. Both are very well respected and they use a minimally invasive method (don't open the peri- orbital bone). We've met with the younger one twice and haven't spoken with the older one yet, but his name has been recommended to us repeatedly by other docs. We hope to have it scheduled and accomplished by the middle of next month. Since we just made this decision, literally over the weekend, the details of timing aren't yet set and may not be till the end of this month.

I like that there are two experienced skull-base surgeons involved, whereas everywhere else has one (with tech or research fellow as partner in the surgery). I also like the more modern hospital here versus the other one we were considering. Depending on timing, I'll go ahead with it here. IF -- big IF -- they cannot schedule me in a timely manner, I may still go elsewhere in the US, but I sure prefer to be here [in Toronto] for a smooth transition and follow-up. And I am comfortable with the surgical choices.

Please pose any pertinent questions, Lou. Nothing is set in stone till I submit to the knife.

Love to you both,
Julie

*   *   *

My brother's response emphasized the urgency of getting it done, as there'd obviously been progression on the follow-up MRI. Time is not on my side.

*   *   *

What a tumultuous couple of weeks! First we were encouraged to consider NOT doing surgery and maybe only doing fractionated radiation. Then my recent MRI showed measurable tumor growth (for the first time) and invasive movement into the optic nerve canal. That brought an about-face consensus from the tumor board that surgery first (and later radiation, only if needed) is the best plan. Surgery will de-bulk, allowing for more room if there's any regrowth in future. It will also allow for a definitive tissue diagnostic analysis. Hopefully (90% chance), it will stabilize my vision loss, which is progressing at an alarming rate just recently.

Much love and appreciation for all that you have done for the two of us on this journey. There's more to come.

Julie

*   *   *

One stepdaughter wrote that she was glad that I have a decision on how to move forward. It was great for her to hear the relief in her dad's voice when they spoke on the phone.

*   *   *

Good morning, C. Thank you for your understanding about my inability to connect. This past week or ten days was surely one of the hardest yet for me. I'm glad it's over. With the new MRI evidence of tumor growth and invasion of my optic canal, the tumor board that met on this Thursday, some of whom were also at the previous tumor board, came to an about-face consensus conclusion: surgery first is the best for my situation.

Now my challenge is getting all my neglected "ducks in a row," and also making a decision about who/where/when. The *when* part needs to be soon and is partly dependent on who and where. The "ducks" are there no matter what, my background lurking to-do list before I face a potentially life-altering and permanently debilitating operation. Sure, we're doing this to save my sight and prevent future brain issues if it's a "grower." But I know there are no guarantees, and the risks are high. The benefits seem to outweigh those, nonetheless. I don't feel I have much of a choice from my perspective, as my right eye seems to grow worse by the day.

I'm so overwhelmed, tired and sometimes depressed. So very tired of being in this tumor paradigm. This has been the biggest distraction I've ever faced. Yet, I must accept that it IS my life, if I am going to move on and pass through it with equanimity, learning to live with the long-term developments. Some days I just don't have the strength to feel like myself any more. I would like to flee. There's nowhere to hide and no rest that is devoid of the truth of the matter.

So, today I will attack my to-do stuff with purpose. I've got to get through the many issues that I still face so I can do this surgery with some semblance of personal peace.

Sending love and hugs,
Julie

*   *   *

Hi, Dear Ones.

Before saying more, you have my deep gratitude for all your support. I feel it in so many ways, hour by hour and day by day. Thank you. At long last, I've something more decisive to share with you.

Since March, I have been seeking a path that resonates with my best healthy outcomes. After gathering many opinions, professional and otherwise, I've decided to have surgery, probably here in Toronto, and hopefully before the middle of next month. Final details are still pending and will be until at least the end of this month, when I next meet with doctors.

We had a slight blip recently when one tumor board met and advised that I consider fractionated radiation alone, as the risk seemed too great for surgery with less likelihood of the good outcomes we seek. We met with the radiation oncologist and even scheduled a mask fitting so I'd be ready to start those thirty treatments. Then at the next tumor board meeting, they did a complete about-face, because my right eye's sight is visibly deteriorating and now the tumor shows measurable growth on the most recent MRI. It's growing into the optic nerve canal. For these reasons, other options (such as fractionated radiation or wait-and-see) are not advised (we have a medical consensus on the matter after much back and forth). I feel like a well-worn tennis ball.

While it's a relief to have a decisive direction, many factors are still up for discussion and scheduling. My hospital preference is based on the two-neurosurgeon team, both very experienced skull-base experts (one with forty years and one with ten).

None of my other options included that "tag team" arrangement. This surgery is very serious and tricky, and it could last 12 hours or more. I like knowing the two can share that potential marathon. I like other things about their proposed procedure too. I'm following my gut, my heart and my head, along with Earl's invaluable input and that of many other supporters and medical types, and it's time to do this thing.

I look forward to seeing each of you soon.

Love and hugs,
Julie

*   *   *

My in-laws wrote to express their admiration of my careful and conscientious pursuit of the right process for me. They are with me in spirit throughout this journey and anxious to hear timing and where I will do it.

*   *   *

My brother and sister-in-law wrote to assure me they think of me a lot: little things. They think it sounds like I am leaning forward into my best possible choices. I am in their consistent thoughts and prayers! So nice to feel lifted this way . . .

*   *   *

Dear friends,

Forgive me if a) I neglected to send you that last status update or b) I already sent it before. Forgive me for anything else I've done or not done in every conceivable category too, won't you please?

Thank you for all your love and support, always, and especially during this time of great personal trial and . . . there's a word-thought not worth repeating! Okay, I'll say "upheaval."

I'm feeling so much sadness lately. It's hard to get down to business on the tasks that are most important to complete before surgery in the middle of next month, and we're hoping for that to happen. Don't know how to get past this part of "it" except to go through it.

I love you all.
Julie

*   *   *

[I wrote a note to Earl.]

Hi, my beloved you.

The lawyer will call me back to quote for my:

- Simple will
- Powers of attorney for health and finance
- Advocate - legal and financial - for life care

Then, if we agree, we can set up an appointment.

Love,
Julie

*   *   *

Dear Dr. Z,

We look forward to our upcoming appointment on Friday at 5 p.m. and would like to complete the steps to schedule a successful operation at that meeting. As you know, we prefer the earliest possible time that we can schedule to operate—and hopefully before the 15th of December. Will I be signing consent forms on Friday?

When I met with the memory doctor (who discovered the tumor) last week, she explained to me that I am "begging for a stroke" now, because of the mass effect and constriction that the tumor is exerting on the internal carotid artery. Though results can never be promised with a guarantee, we know there is a great sense of urgency to have this done as soon as possible.

Given this urgency, we're wondering whether you will be consulting with Dr. G this week so that he will also be up-to-date with my case's particular features and challenges.

We're also wondering if it's possible for me to have a tentative date for the operation before we meet.

We believe that it is a tremendous benefit for us to have the pair of you. Thank you for presenting that operating team strategy when we met. Your stellar reputations precede you both, and we know people who know people who were your patients or medical school colleagues, etc., who have great things to say. This eases our minds quite a lot.

We have the support of our family and friends to be there for me 24/7 when I'm released to the ward after being in the ICU, and later at home. I feel cared for by so many people, including you, Dr. Z.

With vast appreciation,
Julie (and Earl)

*   *   *

[I wrote to my friend.]

Thank you for thinking of me. This week is starting out better than last for my emotional status. Last week was fair to totally sucky for my mood. Now I'm having a persistent deep back/side/tail pain that I just can't figure out and dispel, worse when I sit and no better when I whine -- ha! After two low back fusions, I'm not immune to such developments, but it's been a long, long while since I've had any lingering issues. This one's now with me five days -- enough already!

I've so much to do and feel the pressure of the long (and short) list. Carving away at it all, bit by bit. And meanwhile, meeting with one client this morning by phone, another this afternoon in person. Oh my!

We haven't any further info regarding my brain, except that on Friday one doc we met with said I'm "begging for a stroke" now with the internal carotid artery being constricted by the mass effect of the tumor (latest MRI showed this). Will they be able to release it? Only having the operation will be able to determine that success. I'm counting on YES!

Friday the 27th we meet with the surgeon to set up an operating date, pre-op clearance steps, signing of the papers, etc. That same day, I meet with a lawyer to get my legal ducks in a row. I don't have a Canadian will nor the proper POAs for medical and financial, etc., and I soon will.

I'd rather be sitting by the lake and watching the ducks. How 'bout you? We have our first "sticky" snow. It's light but it's white. I imagine all the smartest ducks have found a warmer lake to spend the winter.

It's so good to feel your thoughts and your supportive care. I am deeply grateful for you.

Wishing you Love and Light,
Julie

*   *   *

My bro wrote to say he was so glad that I am at the point that I can make a plan to take care of this tumor! He's sad that I'm losing my sight, and hope that's at least halted, if not reversed, to some degree. He imagines surgery is scary, but I will be in good hands, and surgery = hope.

* * *

Hi, Fambly.

The Mayo Clinic reached out to me today saying they're holding me a surgery date. I had sent my most recent MRI, and the growth of the tumor since August calls for prompt action, so says the man in white. Harvard is also reaching out to me to confirm to them if I want a date, because they also have my recent MRI.

By Friday (when I meet with the Toronto team) or this weekend I assume I'll have picked a place (hoping for Toronto) and have a mid-month date with the knife.

I have so much work on my plate right now. Perhaps this is good.

Love and hugs,
Julie

* * *

The Brigham & Women's Hospital-Harvard, Boston, surgeon with whom I had consulted in September wrote to ask if it was still my wish to have surgery there, during the following month, with him at the helm of the procedure.

* * *

I responded:

Thank you, Dr. A. The week starting with the 14th would be my preference. And I will not know until Friday or Saturday whether opting to come to B&W-Harvard is a definite plan. My reason is I prefer to have the surgery here in Toronto if they will make it so. I meet with that team on Friday.

If they can't or won't schedule for next month, then I do not intend to wait till the following month or later. So, I'll be in communication with you again first thing over the weekend or on Monday at the latest. I also understand if you cannot hold dates in the schedule for a "maybe" and I'll accept the consequences.

I am deeply grateful for your understanding and patience with me. This is the hardest thing I've ever had to choose to do. It is what it is.

Julie

                *   *   *

Dr. A wrote again, encouraging me to be happy and worry-free. He assured me I will do fine; in Toronto there are fine neurosurgeons and facilities. He wished me the best and full recovery for whatever arrangement suits me.

                *   *   *

Thank you for your email, Dr. Z.

It was very good to meet with Dr. G, though we did not leave with the outcome we anticipated: a date for surgery and a clear agreement on why that is advisable. We listened closely to his concerns and they echoed those of our earlier meetings with you and with Dr. L [the neuro-oncologist].

This information (below) was what I could not produce to share with Dr. G on Friday, and I'm sharing it now, based on review of the actual reports.

Measurements reported by the radiologists on my four MRIs, each in cm:

February : 3.1 x 3.0 x 2.7
May: 3.3 maximum diameter
August : 3.3 maximum diameter
November : 3.4 x 3.1 x 2.9

On Thursday, Dr. C relayed to me this measured growth, from February to November, taken at the November 12 tumor board presentation of my case (the respective changes in the same planes of measurement):

3.07 --> 3.53 and
1.46 --> 1.73 cm

Referring to all of the above figures, based on this amount of growth, at least .3cm and possibly .5cm, I was informed that the tumor may not be a Grade 1 [the slowest growing designation] and this was a strong factor in their recommending surgery first versus radiation, and in doing so quickly.

In our Friday meeting Dr. G was under the impression that the tumor had grown about 1mm in these past nine months; however, that was distinctly different from my understanding coming into the meeting. He indicated he would be consulting with another radiologist to determine as accurate a growth measurement as possible and then advise me if I should be concerned about scheduling a surgery faster than the timing we discussed.

Is there any possibility I will have this new radiologist's assessment by next Monday? I have agreed to let the Mayo Clinic know if I want their O.R. date of the middle of next month by Monday. They're holding this date for me.

I prefer to stay here in Toronto. I prefer to have Team Z-G as my doctors. I also prefer to know that we are all on the same page about tumor growth, urgency of any action, and what action you recommend, based on those factors. Does your recommendation change based on 1mm versus 3-5mm of tumor growth in nine months? We did not leave with the impression that this growth was incorporated into Dr. G's recommended strategy, because he didn't have that understanding prior to the meeting.

We understand clearly that both you and he, and Dr. L, want us to know the likely outcome of some critical portion of tumor remaining in my brain, even under the best of lucky circumstances. That part of our discussion was very clearly communicated, both in words and in visual review of the

MRI pictures. You and he want the best quality of life outcome for me, and I appreciate that so very much.

So please let me know as soon as possible if the growth does change your comfort level with scheduling the surgery. And if so, what do you recommend? Can we do it here in Toronto?

Thank you kindly for your supportive communication and your prompt responses. I appreciate them so very much.

Best regards,
Julie

*   *   *

My sister emailed to empathize with my full plate. She said she felt rather helpless to support me. If she could only be in my shoes, she'd know how very much I do feel her support. We both wish we were closer in proximity to each other, especially at times like these.

My sister prays for me to have hope, strength, healing and courage to face what is coming. She prays that my doctors be given wisdom, knowledge, clarity, assurance, a steady hand and guidance. I am so thankful to have her in my life; she makes me feel confident and thankful that I am loved, by her and by our Creator Who does want the best for me and does have a great plan for the rest of my life!

I am so richly blessed by my siblings!

*   *   *

I have an appointment time with you on your next clinic day, Dr. Z. So, yes, I will see you then.

Yesterday I released the Mayo Clinic O.R. date so they may accommodate another patient.

I look forward to a surgery date with you and Dr. G as soon as possible, though today your office assistant explained to me the schedule is not open yet for those times.

It's been very confusing to me being told at one meeting the tumor board thinks it advisable for me to consider the benefits of radiation alone, the next being told my recent MRI finds growth which indicates this is an urgent matter with another tumor board consensus opinion that surgery should be first, and the following week hearing that it isn't growing fast nor urgent to remove and that (again) surgery may not be the best option for me.

While I believe that everyone has my best outcomes in mind, it boggles my mind to think there is no more consensus than this, especially as regards the growth rate of the tumor. Imagine how that would feel to be in my shoes.

Regards and thanks,
Julie

*   *   *

Another wonderful friend, my Old Pal, wrote to tell me that he chatted briefly with the All-Knowing Entity Upstairs and here, with slight rewording is what She said to tell me: I have several good options. My surgery is based on probability, and my highest probability [of healthy successful outcomes] will be with doctors who have done this type of procedure many successful times. The doctors in Toronto will be outstanding. Earl lives nearby, and so does his extended family; so they can bring flowers and chocolates each day, a win-win situation.

One more thing he added (from the Omnipotent One): I am a fabulous talent and the planet needs me to keep helping others and improving the world, centimeter by centimeter, so I am to do this surgery ASAP and get back to work.

He expressed a little surprise that the All-Knowing Entity Upstairs would be so direct and to the point until he found out She was a Unitarian. He hoped that was not too disappointing to me, a Quaker girl.

My Old Pal had me smiling, as he has many times before.

*　　*　　*

In response to one of the Boston surgical team's note to me, I wrote:

Please let Dr. N know that I am now waiting (and hoping) for an early January operating date here in Toronto, where I live. I meet with the Toronto hospital's surgical team on December 14 and will possibly know more then about a specific plan.

I am glad the tumor is not growing so fast that I have drastic changes in my vision. So far they are slight and only slowly worsening.

I do not look forward to the surgery but am resolved that it's for the best, in spite of the risks. Doing it close to home is my preference, so we may have the ease and support of family and friends.

If my circumstances change and I have a new thought about coming to Boston instead, I will let you know ASAP and also forward visual field exams, etc., at that time.

With great appreciation for your patience and support, Julie

*　　*　　*

One friend wrote to tell me that the past four nights she had "Julie Anxiety." She wanted and needed an update and asked: Was I scheduled for surgery now, an actual date, time, and surgeon? She hoped I am having pain-free days and nights. As she always does, she sent me lots of love and prayers

*　　*　　*

One stepdaughter wrote to say she was sorry that our last appointment sounded so confusing. She couldn't imagine how perplexing it would be to have people giving so many different recommendations to us.

She listed some websites where a person can get second opinions. It usually takes two weeks.

https://econsults.partners.org/v2/(S(zx2qhtndl5ley2ymhgz3vemv))/Doctor/Defau lt.aspx

Vascular experts may be able to comment on the risk of stroke. Also, they say 'contact us' about specialties that aren't listed, here:

https://econsults.partners.org/v2/(S(zx2qhtndl5ley2ymhgz3vemv))/Main/Specialt iesAvailable.aspx

A second site offers second opinions about vascular matters. I might have to come to Boston though for this one:

http://www.massgeneral.org/vascularcenter/appointments/secondopinions.aspx

A third site is for Dana-Farber oncologists, physicians asking for second opinions instead of patients. The idea is to have the two sets of doctors working together.

http://www.dana-farber.org/Partners-Online-Specialty-Consultations.aspx

My stepdaughter thought if I want another opinion, these might be places to go; although more information might be even more confusing. She can understand wanting to go into this understanding as much as possible.

Earl's daughters--all three of them--have been so very supportive of me, and of us, every step of the way. What a blessing they are to us both!

*   *   *

I did request an opinion from one of the above websites, as follows:

I seek an opinion on either 1) fractionated radiation or 2) neurosurgery for a skull- based right sphenoid wing meningioma completely wrapping around my internal carotid artery and pushing aside my right optic nerve.

I've been told my chances are approximately 50% of successful removal of the critical portion of my 3.5cm tumor, the part between carotid and optic nerve. In the case of incomplete removal I will have to have radiation after surgery.

I'm contemplating just having radiation, since there will be no difference in the dose of radiation with or without the removal of the tumor.

Most surgeons (I've met with six experienced teams) recommend surgery, but not all of them. Now it is up to me to decide.

Thank you.
Julie

*   *   *

Thank you for all your help. Monday's surgeon pointed out: we have all the pertinent info we could possibly gather. As far as someone else weighing in with another opinion -- radiation versus surgery -- I'm not clear on the value of that, though I'm not opposed to entertaining it.

It's a very personal decision, weighing all the risks and benefits, and I'm not looking to delegate that to another, no matter how "qualified" he/she may be. It is I who ultimately will decide. I am happy to listen and learn, as always.

Julie

*   *   *

Hi, Lou.

Sorry I've left you uninformed. It's been a tumultuous ride, mostly because I've chosen to stay on it versus scheduling earlier decisive action. I was swayed by one team versus another, then the other versus the previous, etc. I choose to wait for my own "knowing" rather than be convinced by any one of them as to the path I can live with over the coming months and years.

Very close re-examination by multiple folks, surgeons and radiologists, determined the tumor isn't growing at any kind of a measurable rate. I'm not at increased risk for stroke either (as one doctor had suggested), no reason to believe so. I am asked to **consider what outcomes I can and cannot live with over time**; this makes a lot of sense to me. Major stroke (the surgical risk) is one outcome I do not care to embrace. So, I'm still in limbo for a few days or weeks longer.

The neurosurgery teams begin to schedule non-emergent surgeries again after the first of next month, and my O.R. date will entail two of the skull-base neurosurgeons who are coordinating that schedule soon.

I'm still considering radiation alone, to begin around that same time. The rubbery dense makeup of the tumor, visible on CT, MRI, etc., makes them believe that I will have an approximately 50% likelihood of needing fractionated radiation after surgery anyway. With these odds, and the risks and recovery issues from surgery, I'm leaning more toward radiation alone right now.

The plan is for them to give me a surgery date and I can decide right up till that time either *Yea* or *Nay* to go forward.

So, that's my update.

Yesterday I saw a neurologist who will treat me for the headaches, which are most likely NOT directly caused by the meningioma. Go figure!

Hope you both are very well and will be able to enjoy some time off together over the coming weeks.

Love and Hugs, Bro!

Thank you for all your care and concern.
Julie

35

Wrestling with Life in My Dreams

I'm losing the clarity of my dreams, but here's a bit of what I remember.

One had me sitting around a table with a trio of aliens, or angels, who had piercingly blue eyes, beaming eyes that riveted me as these beings spoke to me, telling me my work wasn't done yet. I was left wondering: *Work here? Work where? Are you leaving me or taking me?* No answers . . .

Another dream had me requesting to meet with a person, presumably to discuss my mental health issues, and he travelled a long distance to be with me and discuss these things, but in our meeting I could not voice them. So he left.

Upset and wanting to be able to say what was lurking there on my mental health agenda, I entered a room filled with counseling professionals, all involved with each other and chatting it up. I ascended a podium above them and shouted into their midst:

"My name is Julie and I am suicidal!"

They paused, looked at each other and didn't respond at all to me. They all resumed their chatter, seemingly ignoring my interruption.

Hmmm . . . Weirdly, I knew as soon as I screamed the words that I didn't want to end my life; quite the opposite was true and IS true! So, why had I put on such a show?

These are my two dreams, which now that I typed them, have returned to their original clarity, pretty much. Obviously, I am wrestling with my mortality. What a theme, eh?

I believe dreams are our way of playing out themes and working on them in our unconscious minds. Mine has been busy lately.

36

When Life Gives Me Lemons

I consider how to make lemonade.

I harness the motivation of necessity.

I connect and express appreciation.

I love, the active verb form, in every way I know how. I learn.

I write. I share. I care.

I accept.

I plan. For the worst. For the best.

I glean inspiration from every corner of The Universe.

I bask in the outpouring of support, reflecting it in kind to all who give it, and to all.

Period.

And I thank you. The Particular You. The Universal You.

37

Being Anxious About Anxiety, or Not

Several weeks before I learned anything about having a brain tumor, I was gripped with very strong feelings of anxiety. I may never know why they happened "out of sequence," and I don't try to make meaning of their timing. What I do know is that I learned from the feelings.

In this instance, anxiety came for no identifiable reason. It was not like the kind that follows me stressing over finances, relationship challenges, traumatic memories or the long distance issues of people I love. This was an out-of-the-blue sort of anxiety.

The feeling was cloyingly physical and annoyingly persistent; it came to roost in my body for weeks. I wanted to find my way through and learn some ways of dealing with it until it passed. I was open to many and varied strategies, each of which assisted me in some measure. This is not a chronological list of the tools I used; I layered them and recycled them.

1. Accept. This is a strategy I use whenever circumstances present as adversity in life. I accept. I accept. I accept. From acceptance, happiness can be chosen. I accept that I am anxious. I accept that I don't know why. I accept that I feel what I feel. I accept what is and what isn't, unconditionally. I accept. I accept. I accept.

2. Breathe. Anxiety feels contracted, leaving me less able to expand and open to life. I breathe in. I breathe out. In. Out. Focus on my breath takes me into a relaxing and healing rhythm. I breathe in love and breathe out everything else. In. Out. In. Out. Ahhhhh . . . Breathe.

3. Question. Again and again, when I feel ready to do so, I open myself to receive answers from my deeper, higher and inner wisdom. What am I feeling? Is there a reason? What is on the edge of my consciousness? What may I learn from this? Question.

4. Be here now. The past is the past. The future is imaginary. *AM I being here now?* I ask and ask to assure myself of releasing past and future imaginings. Be here now.

5. Visualize. I hold myself with conscious intention in the light of love. I envision release of all cares, known and unknown, all conceivable ills and concerns. I see myself whole, healthy, happy and filled with a lightness of being. I create the vision. Visualize.

6. Give up. I say aloud, "I give up. I give UP. I GIVE UP!" and I give up, over and over again. I release expectations, even (and especially) those of being free of anxiety. Give up.

7. Ask for help. When anxiety came to roost in me, I made an appointment with my doctor and asked for help. She referred me to a very competent social worker. That was weeks before I learned about my brain tumor, and he continues to be an anchor of support in my life through all these weeks and months of the journey with my ever-evolving knowledge of the tumor. He is an oasis whenever I feel particularly parched. Whether I need him or not, he's there, because I ask. Ask for help.

8. Connect, with purpose. As hard as it is for me to do so, and it is, I connect with others to share my experience with anxiety. Making the connection with THAT purpose assisted me to connect with a deeper one: sharing is caring (for others). I can do that. I've done it before when I shared the experience of my father's end of life. It assists me, as it assists others, to connect, with the purpose of caring. Connect, with purpose.

While these tools worked when my anxiety was of an unknown origin, they've also been helpful to me during more recent times, bouts of fear and concern for "darn good" reasons. I know I will not be anxiety-free every moment of my journey going forward. I also know I will get through. I will cope. I will find comfort and strength in practicing these strategies.

I can be anxious about anxiety, or not.

38

Extending My Reach

Reach out!

Surrounding myself with caring, supportive and positively energetic beings strengthens and reassures me. Feeling the hugs of my loved ones, from youngest to oldest, the nudge of a pet, the smile of a stranger, reaffirms my substance (and lack thereof). I meet Nature's embrace, walk in the spectrum of her changing colors and savor her nourishing delights, both tangible and intangible. As the hand of my beloved reaches out to hold mine, I know the joy of each cherished moment.

Reach in!

Deep resources await me, and I call them into their roles. Emotions keep me real and present. I lean into them and learn from all their dimensions. They give me new insight, new depth of compassion for myself, for others and for all life. I grow my capacity to forgive all potential wrongs. There is no one righteous path; I get this truth. As I choose from all possibilities, I learn there are infinitely more. Counting and cataloguing is futile. In the end, under all the masking layers of hopelessness, blame and fear, there is one prevailing emotion: love, an endless spring of inner peace and boundless joy.

Reach down!

Centering myself firmly upon and within my roots is the kind of intelligence one learns from a tree. I reach deep into my grounding roots. I connect to Source energy, to all who've come before and prepared my path, genetically and energetically. Now I am ready to bend and twist as the wind blows, shed what is broken, recover and grow with the seasons. Even as the tree may whither, its seeds go on. I shall also leave a legacy, a loving and consciously created inheritance for my seed. We shall always be connected through the fibers of our being and our timeless essence.

Reach up!

Skies are a well-stocked pantry of nourishing pleasures. Sun, stars, moon and clouds all teach me that change is never-ending; beauty is a fleeting moment, here and gone, followed by another and another, *ad infinitum*. Within each blank canvas of a day, I may choose how to orchestrate, decorate and embellish its purposes. I may participate fully, creating clear-blue calm or the experience of being buffeted by life's storms. I am a spectator, a watchful observer, noting, "It is what it is," while, "I am that I am." Ah, what the skies have to teach me!

Reaching, grateful, I am at my best.

I am at rest.

39

My Distracting List of Distractions

Theorem A: Distractions keep me from fully living.

Theorem B: Distractions point me toward a fuller life experience.

Theorem C: Discerning what is and what isn't a distraction is itself a distraction.

Theorem D: All of the above coexist within the multi-dimensional mental paradigm of my brain tumor.

My world is filled with distracting thoughts and events, developments and concerns. Critical information flows in and inspires confusion rather than greater clarity.

A lengthening list of questions begs me for answers, or at least for the time to sit with them:

- Is surgery a good idea or not?
- Who, where and what procedure are the best options for surgery?
- Is my tumor's growth rate of concern in the next few weeks and months?
- Will surgery hasten blindness or prevent it?
- Is fractionated radiation a viable alternative to surgery?
- Is my sight disappearing before my eyes ("punny"?) or am I imagining this?
- Will I ever again return to an emotionally stable version of me?

- Do I have time to accomplish the most important things on my agenda before I take potentially life-altering steps forward?
- Will I ever again have the self-directed focus I was once capable of having?
- Should I drop all else in order to see, do, visit and explore all the people, sites and adventures I long to experience, while I still can?
- What are my most important work tasks, my purposes and life-giving roles?
- Is the "promise of tomorrow" a smokescreen I now see through, clearly?
- How may I best prepare for the array of possible tomorrows?
- Is this growing list of questions a distracting diversion or a very purposeful and important exercise for my mind and heart to engage in right now?

You see where this leads me? Straight down the rabbit hole.

Drink this and shrink that.
    Eat that and grow this.
        Enter this door and we'll take care of you.
            Come to tea with the mad ones, if you dare.
            Play croquet with your life.

My Inner Cheshire Cat sits in the tree and grins, as I disappear into each distracting byte.

40

Listening to Trees

"Whoever has learned how to listen to trees no longer wants to be a tree. He wants to be nothing except what he is. That is home. That is happiness." - Hermann Hesse, 1877-1962

From the age of ten, my childhood home bordered a forest, and our yard had many trees. In one of these majestic beauties my brother crafted a tree house that was more like a tree perch, actually. Two long boards nailed into the branches provided a surface where we sat or stretched out to relax. Such was the extent of our "house," ample space for our youthful imaginations.

By age twelve, my brother had turned fifteen and lost his fascination with the tree house. It became my favorite place to climb and daydream alone. I found peace in that happy place, feeling safe in the company of my tree friends. Their strong arms held me as I grew into adolescence.

Listening to trees, I learned *to want to be me*. I listened to the still small voice within, my internal compass. I learned to follow and trust it. I "tree-meditated" daily.

Perhaps this is why I long for daily walks in nature these days, my time to be among the trees. Sometimes even now, it is far easier to go to a tree with my problems than to another human being. When I'm feeling lowest, I have the least ability to share my status with my fellow humans. My need is greatest, yet I am often unable to invite others in. I struggle to ask for the compassionate presence that could lighten the burdens I carry.

The normal and natural thing, for me, is to seek the silent company of trees, their acceptance, strength and lack of judgment. Trees don't expect me to make life- altering decisions. Trees don't press me to show up any way other than *as I am*.

With trees I can share my many misgivings. And, I sure do have them! Whatever I choose for my tumor's direction, there are scary and unforeseen outcomes and possibilities. I walk among the trees and contemplate my pressing questions.

- What if I'm physically compromised? Major stroke means lost independence.
- What if I'm mentally afflicted, unable to think properly and work productively?
- What if I suddenly go blind? Even gradual loss of sight already frightens me.
- What if my emotional resilience is stretched beyond its limits? Sometimes I wonder if this isn't already my truth.
- Will I ever seem like ME again?

Trees, my dear forest friends, can you show me how to come home to me now, how to want to *be* me, at home and happy with my self, tumor and all?

I'm listening.

41

This Is It -- a Decision!

Knowing is just that: *knowing*.

Today, while speaking with a friend on the phone, I realized:

> ***I know. Wow. Finally. I know what choice***
> ***has me feeling the most peace.***

At last I know where my heart leads me after so many months on a tumultuous ride through consultation and consideration, weighing of the facts, risks and benefits.

Every step of the way, I chose to stay on the roller coaster of indecision rather than schedule an earlier action.

Doing nothing with my tumor is not a responsible option; on this the many skilled professionals agree. Most of them also say there is no one "right" choice in my case; it's up to me to choose how I will move forward in peace.

So, week after week, I held my decision in the Light, let my head mull over the many gathered facts and waited for my heart's clear leading.

Over a span of many months, I was informed by one team of doctors, swayed by another, then sought opinions from a third, a fourth and so on. Back and forth, forward and back, I have arrived at this point. Whew.

I consciously chose to wait for my own "resolved knowing" rather than be convinced by any one of the experts. They're right; only I can decide the path I must live with over the coming months and years.

This past week I was coached well, with the surgeon saying I can make the choice in my own time; neither she nor any other can do it for me. No matter which way I go, I may have some regrets later. She asked me to consider which results I can and cannot live with, both immediately and over time.

Her strategy makes a lot of sense to me. Major stroke (roughly a 5% surgical risk) is one possibility I do not care to embrace. Sudden blindness as a result of surgery (an approximated 10% risk) is the other least appealing outcome.

The apparently rubbery and dense makeup of the tumor, visible on CT-angiogram and MRI, leads this doctor's multi-disciplinary team to believe that I would have about a 50% likelihood of needing fractionated radiation after surgery anyway.

Here's why: It's very doubtful that full resection of the unwanted mass is possible, and the critical part of the tumor may be left behind to grow and continue its adverse effects on my optic nerve, and ultimately on both optic nerves.

With these odds, and the risks and recovery issues from surgery, I will opt for fractionated radiation. Today I began the steps to make that happen ASAP. This treatment will mean seven weeks of daily (Monday-Friday) short visits to the hospital, lots of subway schlepping or car trips to and fro. I can handle that, no matter how unappealing the prospect of snow, ice and wintry bustle may seem. We are entering that bitter season.

It will be around six months till we know the success of the treatments, as it takes that long for potential swelling, a side effect of radiation, to subside. I am visualizing 100% restoration of my vision loss and sight stabilization over the long road ahead: 40+ more years of great health and sharp eyes.

Another thing the doctor mentioned is that recent statistical data, collected over the last fifteen years (versus the previous twenty-five to thirty years), indicates no increased risk of brain cancer after radiation, using the newest techniques, when compared with the general population. This also has me breathing with some relief.

So, this is it. I have a clear path ahead. There may be some unforeseen pitfalls and bogeymen, undesirable side effects, such as nausea and hair loss. None of those seem as daunting to me as the weight of making this choice.

Now it's made. I can "try that on" and get used to it, another opportunity for acceptance and gratitude.

As I looked for a bit of inspiration to face the road ahead, I found these well-worn words:

> "You gain strength, courage and confidence by every experience in which you really stop to look fear in the face. You are able to say to yourself, 'I have lived through this horror. I can take the next thing that comes along.' You must do the thing you think you cannot do."
>
> - Eleanor Roosevelt, 1884-1962

It is what it is! This is it! I did it!

*   *   *

Hi, Dr. Z.

I've decided to proceed with fractionated radiation, and I called Dr. L's office to set up the next steps. I am hopeful to begin as soon as they can accommodate me in the schedule.

I cannot thank you (and Dr. G) enough for your ongoing support and attention. Your thoughtful and patient presentations of all the facts, risks, benefits and "logic of choice" pertaining to my outcomes have been immeasurably helpful to me. Thanks so very much.

With best wishes for your happiness! Julie (and Earl)

*   *   *

Greetings to my radiant pals!

I hope all are well and enjoying a variety of family and friendly gatherings over this Holiday period. Merry Christmas to all who celebrate the day! Peace on Earth begins in the heart of each one. May peace and love be yours, mine and ours.

After these many months of medical testing, consultations, and holding my decision in the Light, I've decided on fractionated radiation as a first (and hopefully only) treatment of my skull-based tumor. I am at peace with that direction and will soon know how the seven weeks of daily zapping will be scheduled. Doing nothing is not an option; on this the many "knowing professionals" are in agreement.

I was coached well this past week, with the surgeon saying I must decide; she cannot do it for me. No matter which way I go, I may have some regrets later. This being the case, she asked me to consider what outcomes I can and cannot live with over time; this makes a lot of sense to me. So, I remained in limbo for a bit longer to contemplate. The key factors in this decision are:

- Surgical risks that I cannot embrace, 5% major stroke (or death) and 10% immediate blindness
- The rubbery, dense nature and position of my tumour with only a 50% chance of successful complete resection, meaning I would have subsequent fractionated radiation anyway, after the surgery
- Better recent statistical data, collected over the last 15 years (versus previous 25-30 years), indicating no increased risk of brain cancer after radiation (with newest techniques) when compared with the general population

Thank you, each and all, for the tremendous support you provide to me. I love you and feel your love each day, such a blessing and a source of strength to me. I look forward to seeing you soon.

Love and Light,
Julie

*   *   *

My friend wrote to celebrate my great news! She was so happy that I decided on the best plan for my treatment. She couldn't imagine how grueling the last year has been for me, making this decision.

She thinks, and I agree, I'm very fortunate in so many ways, including having many options available, plus having the luxury to take the time I needed to come to a decision.

She thanked me for the happy update and sent lots of energy and light, now and going forward!

I can feel the love!

*   *   *

I wrote to my buddies:

Please release all Julie Anxiety and embrace the Peace and Good Will of this special time.

My love to you! See you "on the other side" of this radiation therapy. Julie

*   *   *

To my Quaker friends/Friends, I wrote:

I'm starting fractionated radiation next Tuesday and will be making daily trips into the Toronto downtown hospital to get those treatments, M-F, for the next seven weeks. Looking forward to emerging victorious and travel-primed.

I feel relief having made this decision, glad to be avoiding the potential pitfalls of surgery that loomed large, and still needing radiation afterwards. It's a rubbery little bugger that's very intimately involved in my brain junk.

They predict a 90-95% successful outcome, so that my vision will be preserved as is and possibly even restored to its former clarity.

Focusing now on peace, health and renewal, a new "me-ness" in the New Year.

Love and hugs,
Julie

*   *   *

Hi, J.

I leave momentarily to get my radiation mask fitted and the CT and MRI mapping of the tumor in the machine where I'll be zapped. Then it'll be about ten days till that's ready for me to start the treatments. A long journey ahead.

Merry Christmas and Happy New Year!

Love,
Julie

*   *   *

This was a Holiday letter I wrote to my in-laws living in Massachusetts:

My health "story" took a sharp turn this past year when I learned that I have a skull- based meningioma, a benign brain tumor that actually isn't IN the brain tissue, but it's well established in some prime real estate there.

It is pushing my right optic nerve, causing some gradual sight deficits, and also is wrapped around the internal carotid artery.

We did lots of investigation about the path to take for treatment and finally concluded that fractionated radiation was my best choice. Surgery was another option but not one I wanted to risk (the risks are quite unsavory -- major stroke, death, sudden blindness) when total resection of the critical portion of tumor is unlikely; I would need radiation anyway in that case. I begin the seven weeks of daily M-F treatments this PM.

I never planned to learn so much about the brain, meningiomas and treatments, but here I am, informed and resigned, and also very hopeful. There is a 90-95% chance this will curtail the tumor's growth and a small chance it may restore the sight I've lost (which so far isn't too bad -- could be much worse).

I'm thankful for all the support and resources available to me and for living in a time when such treatment is available, increasingly safe and well tested on scores of others.

This year will be a better one. Hopefully, within a few months, we'll be able to focus on fun stuff and not be so tumor-driven. Most of our travels in 2015 were to consult with specialists and/or to inform family members about my dilemma, which I preferred to do face-to-face with some of them.

You two take care and please know that I think of you often. I love you and treasure my memories of times together.

Joyfully!
Julie

*   *   *

Another email to friends went like this:

The whole week went pretty well. Yesterday was a morning radiation session because each Friday the doctor sees me, and all others were mid-PM.

On Thursday I took the subway, and that's my favorite way to commute, as I suspected it would be. I can sit quietly and read or do a crossword puzzle and not have to be a stop-start-in-the-city car passenger. There is no smooth way to go there via car, and traffic adds another element I prefer not to have to deal with, let alone relying on others to drive.

So, hip, hip, hooray! I made it through treatment Number 4 and only 26 to go. It's a weird experience being strapped down tightly by my hard mesh face mask, but the whole procedure is done very quickly, I really don't mind. In and out and back home till another day. While downtown I'm planning to coordinate with some friend visits, an art gallery trip, etc., if that feels right after I get more into this subway trip groove.

I can smell the radiation. That's kind of weird. I've always had a very acute sense of smell, and lo and behold, I'm one of the few who can smell it.

Love and Oxidation (that's how the radiation kills the tumor!), in the Light,
Julie

*   *   *

Hi, all!

I've completed my ninth treatment and am doing very well. Fatigue and mild headaches are my only issues, but I'm not sure I can blame the headache on the treatment, since I had that before. I don't get much else done but the daily commute there and back, but right now that's my primary job. I accept that.

Have a great weekend. The sun is shining on us right now. HURRAY! Love and Light, hugs too!

Julie

*   *   *

Hi, all. I'm delighted to report I'm halfway done with my 30 radiation treatments today. Woohoo! Planting my victory flag at the top of this mountain and ready to slide down.

It could be wishful thinking, but I'm noticing some visual improvement in the last two days.

Hope springs eternal.
Hugs all around, love,
Julie

*   *   *

Dear, Dear L and family,

I've thought of you so often lately. And I hope your health is being extra well these days.

I'm doing fairly well. The treatments are almost two-thirds complete with no obvious side effects other than fatigue.

Right now I'm dealing with my second head cold in the span of two weeks. I had four days with no symptoms and then it came back extra strong. So, I'm dealing with that as I come and go, daily, via the subway to receive the radiation (which only takes about twenty minutes in all once I'm in the room). Every Friday I also see the doctor, so that takes longer. And I'm leaving shortly, so I had better get out of my jammies and into some warm clothes.

We have snow, but it's supposed to be fairly mild, hovering around freezing and then climbing over the weekend. I'm ready for spring to arrive.

Love and Light, Hugs and Hope!

Julie

*   *   *

Hi, M and P. Thank you for checking in. Today will make twenty treatments, two- thirds of the way done with this bitch. LOL.

For the past several days I've been uber-sick with a head cold. Snot, snot, snot what I'd rather be doing, but IT IS WHAT IT IS! I'm doing my best to rest and recuperate, and I must go to the scheduled treatments, no matter what! And so I do that. I'd like to think I'm turning the corner. Eyes aren't quite as red and weepy, nose more stuffed than runny. Is that progress? Anyway, this too shall pass.

Love and hugs coming at you -- no germs; I'm keeping all of those for myself!
Julie

*   *   *

Six more treatments!!!
Thank you for all your great energy and support.
Love and HUGS!
Julie

*   *   *

I am doing well! Fatigue is the main side effect. Just a little hair loss around the sideburn area, which I didn't even notice till the doctor pointed it out to me. HA! I'm looking forward to the liberating feeling of not having the daily trek to and from the hospital. Whew! It will be six months till my next MRI. It takes that long for the slow- growing tumor cells to turn over, which is when they actually die. Then, if there is no growth in evidence, it will be one year till the next MRI. Woot woot!

Love you, bro! Thank you for all your support.

Julie

*   *   *

Mom, would you mind people knowing about your radiation, now that it's over?

Valerie

(To this I responded that it would be okay, so Val "outed" me on Facebook, as you'll see below.)

*   *   *

Hi, Dr. L.

I forgot to ask one question last week when I visited with you. When may I resume taking the many and varied supplements that I used to incorporate into my daily routine? I was advised to stop any antioxidants and they're mostly, or all, in that category. Is it advisable to wait till the next MRI results are assessed in August?

Many thanks again for your kind attention and support,

Julie

*   *   *

He responded that now my radiation was done, there were no concerns about anti- oxidants. I could go ahead and resume my prior supplements.

*   *   *

[posted to Facebook]

Tomorrow, my beautiful mother takes on her 30th and final radiation treatment for the meningioma that pushes upon her right optic nerve and surrounds her carotid artery. I can't begin to describe how proud I am of her. Julie, Mom, you are my greatest inspiration. Thank you for teaching me so patiently how to love and be loved. Your strength, perseverance, and ability to continue laughing from your heart throughout this process are just some of the many reasons I admire you more than you could ever know. Your example guides my every day, Mom. I cannot wait to celebrate with you in person, but for now, I celebrate with you in spirit from thousands of miles away.

I love you forever.
Valerie

* * *

Hi, V. I'm pleased with the week I had, feeling so good to accomplish ANYTHING. Lately, I sure haven't done much in that category except the one BIG thing: all thirty of the radiation treatments. I'm having fairly constant headaches, which may be from the tumor swelling, but nothing too severe. They had been improving in frequency and intensity prior to this past week, so I think they will again. By mid- week next week, all should start to improve, especially fatigue. I'm counting on that. Julie

* * *

My friend wrote to ask how I was doing. She thought of me the whole previous week, and hoped that evidence of the radiation therapy's effectiveness continues to evolve. She hoped I relished my first free Monday in almost two months. She asked me to please let her know how things are whenever I step off Cloud 9 for a minute!

Such a dear friend . . .

* * *

Dearest, Darlingest, Delightfulest, Bestest B,

I'm doing well. Just reached my fatigue peak day, one week post-treatment, and I'm glad it's supposed to get less from here on in, as that's been my biggest side effect. I have been relishing every moment of freedom from the daily three-hour (or more) hospital trek.

And, amidst all, there are lots of "storms" going on around me in others' lives and I am feeling like the hub of a wheel (eye of the storm?) while mindfully, consciously, and sometimes humorously being the observer of my life.

Bottom line: I'm doing great and tremendously positive about my present and future. I started working on projects that I'd put on hold -- yay! -- and just this weekend picked up on exercise again after barely being able to drag myself around (let alone put in extra walking or physical therapy routine).

I'm quite excited to do all these things and more just as soon as I am able. Taking it slow.

HUGS and LOVE,
Julie

*   *   *

Very wiped out, K. Thank you for checking in. I'm okay, just profoundly tired and very gradually adding things into my daily life again. Very relieved to be done with the daily trek to and from the hospital, a three-hour trip.

It will be six months till the next MRI to assess growth/death/shrinkage of the tumor. Next month I'll have my follow-up in-depth visual assessment, which may be early in the scheme of things. Why the MRI is scheduled so far out is because it's such a slow-growing tumor, it takes that long for the irradiated cells to turn over and attempt to divide and that's when each cell actually dies, presumably. Also, for the first four months, the tumor can appear larger due to swelling from the radiation. That enlargement is temporary.

I lost some hair (thinned and less sideburn hair), lost my ability to taste most things (don't know for sure why this happened, though it could be the sinus issue I've now had for three or more weeks, or it could be a cranial nerve issue) and I look older.

Otherwise, other than fatigue, I'm doing great and very optimistic. Hugs and love to you both,

Julie

*   *   *

Exhaustion continues to be my biggest issue right now and I'm simply not able to get the hours of sleep I seem to need, this week worse than last for various reasons beyond my control.

And I've had the "sinus syndrome of 1000 tissues" for about a month, now wondering if I'll always have it. For the longest time I couldn't taste anything and wondered if that would ever come back. It mostly did.

I never had much of an issue with cough but my nose is a never-ending source of clear secretions. I also can't sing properly (a new development related to this issue).

Julie

*   *   *

I received some very good news today. My visual screening tests and retinal scans and photos showed much improvement since the previous ones (June and September). All great results, almost normal: 'borderline' versus previous 'out of the normal range.'

I was hoping for this, naturally, after thirty radiation treatments, but had no expectation of this much improvement this early after their conclusion three weeks ago.

My next MRI isn't scheduled till late August, because radiation can cause artificial tumor enlargement due to swelling. So . . . I'm very pleased and hoping now for total restoration into the NORMAL range for my right eye by then (when I'll also have vision assessed again).

Fatigue is still an issue for me, and I know this too shall pass. Thank you for your tremendous support.

So much love!
Julie

*   *   *

In response, my friend wrote to suggest that I get a T-shirt "Almost Normal." So fun!

*   *   *

My professor friend congratulated me on my great news. He added, and I agree, that it is amazing how we take for granted things like eyesight, hearing, walking, and just being alive.

He would like to tell this to some of his students who worry so much about papers and tests, but he also knows it is natural to worry about these things and likely they would not understand anyway. One must have a life-threatening or life-altering experience to truly understand.

Perhaps he is correct.

*   *   *

Hi, K.

Last week, on Monday, I had a visual field / retina / optic nerve exam with the neuro-ophthalmologist who has been following me since June. I was really at my low point physically and energetically, so it was a wonderful surprise to find out I had such great results so soon after radiation was complete. My right optic field was "borderline" or just a bit off the normal range, way better than "outside normal range" by worsening degrees as was noted in June and September. Additionally, the retinal and optic nerve photos, which can pick up electron microscopic level variations, had returned to the "green zone" -- essentially very fine.

This is amazing news, much earlier than I would have expected, according to the neuro-oncologist's postponing of any further MRI for six full months. And, it means not just halting of the decline, but real progress towards full vision health. Hip, hip, hooray! I had been telling Earl, "Either I'm getting used to the diminishing sight or it's actually better now." I now have concrete evidence of the same.

By Wednesday, my energy started returning too, and I'm up to my usual long walks and stair climbing (we have two flights in our home, climbed frequently) without feeling like I've climbed Mt. Everest.

I'm really so happy about all these things. Life is returning to some semblance of normalcy. Headaches are also almost a thing of the past, and good riddance!

Thank you for all your support and healthy wishes.

Love and hugs,
Julie

*   *   *

Hi and Howdy, everyone!

Whatever you may be doing, wherever you may be, I invite you to join me in a little happy dance. Be careful if you are operating heavy machinery, however. I don't want to be responsible for any injuries today. Dance, dance, dance!

I have joyous news after visiting with the radiation oncologist today. Having taken an MRI of my brain on August 19th, the doctor appointment today was to "interpret" that scan and assess the success of my thirty radiation treatments, completed six months ago.

TADA!! There is NO growth and a very slight measure of shrinkage, which means the treatments are a success! My next MRI will be in one year. Why such slow shrinkage, you might ask? Because it's such a slow-growing type of tumor (meningioma) that the cell turnover (when they attempt to divide and grow) is so slow. And that is when the cell dies, when its injured DNA (from the radiation) cannot successfully divide to make a new cell. So, itty bitty bit by itty bitty bit, this tumor will shrink over the years to come.

I thank you each and all for your patience, your superlative support and abundant health-infused energy, and most of all, for all the love.

Hugging your essences, with so much gratitude. Julie

42

Christmas Eve -- Present, Masked and Mapped

"Lie here on the scanner table and we'll fit your mask first."

This is how I began my adventure into fractionated radiation, with a mask fitting. The technicians worked hard to find the best fit for a support to cradle the back of my head. They explained how critical it is for that piece to fit snugly to the base of my skull and top of my back. When treatments begin, there must be no chance of me moving in the slightest from the position where these measurements were made.

"Great, that's perfect. How does it feel? Now, lie very still as we bring the mesh over to fit it to your face. It will be warm and wet. Close your eyes and breath normally but please don't move your head at all during this next five minutes while we smooth the mesh over your face to shape it. It will dry solidly by then and we'll remove it briefly to cut holes for your eyes. It's very important that you not move at all during that time."

I listened carefully and did my best to obey these commands. I certainly didn't want any slip-ups in the process that would determine the exact volume of my tumor and how much radiation it receives.

"Okay. Here we come with the warm, wet mask."

What an odd sensation to have the mask over me as they pressed it firmly against my entire face, chin and hairline on all sides! It was strange but not frightening and the two techs spoke soothingly. I breathed normally and held as still as still could be.

Then they coached me to stay very still while they cut holes for my eyes and returned the hardened mesh mask to my face so they could perform a CT-scan while the mask was in place. This, coupled with a subsequent MRI scan in another room of the hospital, supplied the critical information medical physicists would use to calculate my dosing of radiation.

Coming and going from the hospital I noted the many individuals who have roles as patient, family member, friend or caregiver. We're all a part of this great machine of hope and healing, wheels and cogs turning at our respective speeds and positions.

One young woman, her head covered with a wrapped scarf, helped me find my way from the subway exit to the hospital entrance. I told her I would soon start my seven weeks of treatments. She told me she has thirty more days of her own. When I mentioned my brain tumor, she didn't volunteer her own diagnosis. I didn't ask.

I am present, masked and mapped. Christmas Eve is a great day to begin again.

43

Making My Own Path

"Walk across the snow and there is your path."

- Thomas Merton, 1915-1968

Dr. Z wouldn't choose for me. No one can.

The following quote has sometimes been attributed to Plato:

"An unexamined life is not worth living."

In fact, these words come from *Plato's Apology*, Plato's recollection of Socrates' speech, made at his trial after he chose death rather than being exiled from Athens or committed to a life of silence.

I thank both of these philosophers for making this provocative quote accessible to me, as it is applicable to my life circumstances. If there is one thing I've surely been doing these past several months, since discovering my meningioma, it's examining my life. For this opportunity, I am deeply grateful.

"One can choose to go back toward safety or forward toward growth. Growth must be chosen again and again; fear must be overcome again and again."

- Abraham Maslow, 1908-1970

I do admire Maslow and look to him for inspiration. In my particular case, there is no option to "go back toward safety." I cannot undo the facts or find safety in ignoring them. There is only going forward in one direction or another. All along this journey I've chosen to look fear in the face and let my inner compass lead the way. I must choose again and again and again to be open to the path forward. And I do.

Sometimes I ask myself: How would one live each day as though it was one's last? And the answer comes clearly through: In gratitude, always and all ways. To live each of my days as though it is my last, I will live in gratitude.

It's my choice to give voice to my inner voice, thoughts and fears, to the ups and downs, ins and outs of my journey. This is my chance to share whatever it is that I want others to know, to express myself fully to those I love and care about.

There are no guarantees. Diagnoses that inspire us to think of death as a real possibility create that clarity like nothing else can. "Coming out" from wherever I may be playing it safe takes vulnerability and courage. Yet, that is how I will step into my greatest essence.

"Let me not die while I am still alive."

- Jewish prayer

Now *there's* a prayer to inspire some deep thought! I am still alive and ready to live so much more of life. Hallelujah for that!

My position is not my disposition. Yes, I may have a brain tumor, but that doesn't mean I have to let it ruin my life. I can choose to let it inspire my life. I can choose to dedicate myself to great self-care.

When an airline steward says, "Put your own oxygen mask on first before you place one on your child," the important takeaway is this: Look out for yourself, because you can't help anyone else if you are not able to breathe. This lesson is applicable to all facets of life. The most successful people know this fact.

Saying "No" to many things means saying "Yes" to my priorities. Acting on my priorities is the kind of self-care that creates more life in my days.

Knowing that I'm acting on my priorities is like life-giving oxygen to my cells. It's breathing more deeply of the truths that are most important to me.

When gazing into a glass prism, what one sees depends on how the glass is turned. Isn't that the truth about my life going forward? I can choose to see new colors, shapes and horizons; openings for new growth, challenges and opportunities. On the other hand, I could choose to feel bound and constrained by imagined unhealthy outcomes, restrictive thoughts and worries. Prism or prison? The choice is mine.

The journey is what it is, so I might as well enjoy.

Love is the most powerful medicine. I can choose to love myself, as I am, and to love others as they are. Perhaps I don't fit exactly my own model of "Ideal Me." So what? I can love the differences and just appreciate who I am at this moment, *without trying to change the Now Me*. This is so liberating! Every time I give myself, or another, unconditional love, I open myself to let the Light pour into me and through me.

Every direction I look, I see light, wholeness, connection and love. Love. Love.

Then, in the space of not trying to change another, my situation or me, I spontaneously do change into the person who is capable of unconditional love. Evolution of that natural sort is "Viktory, Frankly." Yes, it's my little name pun inspired by his quote.

> "When we can no longer change a situation, we are challenged to change ourselves."
>
> - *Man's Search for Meaning* (1946)
> by Viktor Frankl, 1905-1997

Each of us, when we live with eyes and hearts wide open, meet with opportunities to transform seeming negativity into positive experiences. When we encounter a challenging person or situation, we may think reactively: "How can I make this quickly go away?" How different life can be when we consciously hold this thought instead: "How may I transform this experience into Light? Truth? Hope? Love? How may I harness this situation to make a lasting change in me?" The Universe sends gifts in many, varied and unusual guises. Am I ready to receive them? Are you?

I wonder if you see the grains of Truth and Light in this passage, as I do: Rabbi Shimon, who was the author of the Zohar, once hid in a cave to escape persecution. He left the cave fourteen years later with atrophied limbs and skin covered with sores. Others cringed at the sight of him and were moved to tears of pity, but the Rabbi responded to them, saying, "If I wasn't as I am, I wouldn't be who I am."

Living through troubles and challenges creates in me (and in you) a greater capacity to handle them. Greater women and men than I have recognized this.

> "If I had a formula for bypassing trouble I would not pass it around. Trouble creates a capacity to handle it. I don't embrace trouble; that's as bad as treating it as an enemy -- but I do say meet it as a friend for you will see a lot of it, and had better be on speaking terms with it."
>
> - Oliver Wendell Holmes,
> American Jurist and Supreme Court Justice,
> 1809- 1894[5]

Loving All That Is, unconditionally, I evolve into the Witness Me, who isn't trying to change another of the other facets of Me. Witness Me is an observer, a centered Self who can notice that which is happening without investing emotions, without trying to direct or produce any other outcome other than What Is.

I have heard some say that Soul is the Witness. It's not important to me to call it one thing or another thing; the more I identify with the Witness Me, the more interesting it is to observe my life.

---

[5] Retrieved on December 1, 2017, http://wist.info/author/holmes-jr-oliver-wendell/

Another aspect of my evolution is this: When I agree with What Is, and release any power my circumstances may have over me -- rather than engaging with them as an adversary -- the lack of resistance allows me to be "friendly" with What Is.

Agreement is akin to disarmament, and I can follow the Path of Least Resistance going forward, so much easier than battling my way through these circumstances. I accept. I agree. I am one with What Is without opposition. Ease and peace are mine.

Does this mean I ignore or avoid my feelings that arise, such as hurt, anger, grief or fear? Not at all! I can turn toward them, fully, with great self-compassion, and explore each feeling with all the curiosity Witness Me can muster (she's VERY curious).

With practice, I realize I am safe to explore each uncomfortable feeling. I'll live through the pain or discomfort of each one, and I can trust myself to not judge Me for feeling them. These emotions are perfectly human, normal and natural, especially for one facing a serious diagnosis! They may not be pleasant, but I'll be fine with each of those feelings.

My curiosity will help me to explore and learn what each feeling is like for Me. It's a new experience from which I may learn quite a lot. Doing so, I gain the knowledge that I can cope, healthily, and do better in future, all through this self-exploration and experience. Witness Me observes the strength I develop as I hold myself open to a full spectrum of feelings.

Perhaps you can relate to my desire to feel control of outcomes. Do we ever really control how things will turn out? My life has definitely been graced with unexpected outcomes, whether or not I set particular goals for myself. I've reached many goals, but they're often quite different -- and far more wondrous -- than I even imagined them to be.

Intentions may have been integral to my achievements, but I've learned many times over that having intentions is one thing, while holding them too tightly is another.

Happiness, relaxation, ease and mindfulness hinge far more often on me holding on loosely to any particular outcome; that is, being willing to relinquish control.

So, Witness Me notices my desire to have some control, and the urges do arise from time to time. I can witness without doing anything to "take over" and follow that controlling urge. I can notice, acknowledge and then give credit to the beauty of The Universe with all its unpredictable, growing, changing and uncontrollable aspects. Sunrises and sunsets are such great examples. We let them happen. We enjoy their many colors. I may take action to assure I'm there for the sunset or sunrise, but I wouldn't dream of trying to control it. It is perfect in its natural unfolding.

In life, I can choose my actions, based on my preferences, working with others to realize our goals, and I can do so without attachment to specific outcomes, trusting the process, knowing my intentions are for the best: to be helpful, to do good, to create harmony and beauty along the way. How will it all turn out? That's part of the great mystery of life. It's okay not to know. I trust What Is to be just fine. Perfect, in fact.

In addition to choosing my actions, I can choose my perspective. I can look at anything (for instance, a "serious" brain tumor diagnosis) and decide what it's going to mean, if indeed it shall mean anything whatsoever! I can choose and choose and choose again, until my perspective is one of peace.

My companion throughout this journey is Grief.

> "She was no longer wrestling with the grief, but could sit down with it as a lasting companion and make it a sharer in her thoughts."

> - George Eliot, a.k.a. Mary Anne Evans,
> 1819-1880, English novelist and editor,
> *Middle-march*, bk. 8, ch. 80 (1871),
> of Dorothea Brooke.[6]

---

[6] Retrieved on December 1, 2017, https://books.google.ca/books

Why Grief? I am no longer the person who doesn't know about my meningioma, who doesn't know that a treatment of one sort or another, with its accompanying risks, looms ahead. I am Brain Tumor Me now, and being that person means I grieve for the other Julie, the person I was before. Anyone who receives a serious diagnosis has a life-defining Before and After, the former being a more carefree existence and the latter being the informed and weighty one, with its new dimensions of feelings, including Grief.

> "I myself stand in need of the arms of my own kindness."
>
> - Ram Dass[7]

And I do. I hold myself with loving kindness in an embrace of total acceptance of What Is.

> "Rebellion against your handicaps gets you nowhere. Self-pity gets you nowhere. One must have the adventurous daring to accept oneself as a bundle of possibilities and undertake the most interesting game in the world-making the most of one's best."
>
> - Harry Emerson Fosdick, 1878-1969[8]

Writing this book, little chapter by little chapter, is one of the ways I am making the game interesting. As I look at what's ahead, the decision and its consequences, I know there may always be some lingering questions about "what is best." As I've done at other crossroads in my life, when very serious choices lay ahead, I say to myself, "I may not know if my choice will be the best, but I do know that I will make the very best of my choice."

My brain tumor has been a great motivator for establishing and re-establishing personal priorities. It has motivated me to ask myself:

---

[7] Reprinted with permission from RamDass/RamDass.org

[8] Statement of 1937 or earlier, as quoted in *The New Speaker's Treasury of Wit and Wisdom* (1958) edited by Herbert Victor Prochnow

- Where do I want to be in relationship to the people I hold most dear?
- How may I address any gaps in these relationships?
- What is my relationship with The Earth and how may I take more responsibility for its stewardship?
- Do I honor the best in myself, fulfilling my own creative capacity?
- When life draws to a close and I am at rest for the very last time, will I have important regrets, or will I know that I have aligned my life according to what is most precious to me?
- How may I make choices now that help me achieve that kind of peace?

I am grateful for this chance to examine with care the Who, What, When, Why and Where of my life.

> "Today, we fill our mind and vision with thoughts that we love, visions of possibility and the life we are meant to live."

> - Mary Morrissey[9] Yes! What *she* said!

Sometimes I have my doubts. I prefer not to have brain surgery. I prefer not to have radiation. I prefer not to have a meningioma growing on the base of my skull and invading my optic nerve canal, wrapping around my internal carotid artery.

> "Our doubts are traitors and make us lose the good we oft might win. By fearing to attempt."

> - Lucio, Act I, Scene IV,
> *Measure by Measure* (c.1603),
> William Shakespeare, 1564-1616[10]

---

[9] Reprinted, with explicit permission, from Mary Manin Morrissey's newsletter, a product of LifeSOULutions That Work LLC

[10] Retrieved on December 1, 2017. https://www.values.com/inspirational-quotes/ 4052-our-doubts-are- traitors-and-makes-us-lose-the

I have doubts about my best path forward. Are my doubts traitors or are they the signposts pointing the way to my best outcome?

Let us now pause while I ask the spirit of William Shakespeare about this matter.

<Pause>

Will (my channelled version of the Bard) says, "Maybe yes and maybe no. Maybe someone else wrote that bit for which I'm famous." Ha! Doubt infused with doubt. What fun!

> "A rock pile ceases to be a rock pile the moment a single person contemplates it bearing within them the image of a cathedral."
>
> - Antoine de Saint-Exupéry, 1900-1944, author of *The Little Prince*[11]

I get to choose what I will make of this brain tumor rock pile and any future rock pile in my life. Giving it positive energy, consciously chosen, and sharing that energy with others, is one of the ways I make the best of my situation. Can I envision the tumor as something as beautiful as a cathedral? Hmmm, not likely. But I can envision my outcomes and results, my future experience, inspired by the tumor in my head, as cathedral-like.

Choice. This is one of the greatest gifts of life. I may choose how I will be with What Is. I may choose whether and how I will grow, what I will be inspired to create and to give to others. Each moment holds a new opportunity to bring light, to bring joy, to bring connection. Each moment is an opportunity to expand and deepen my quest for more understanding. Every single moment can be fuel for my growth. What I find waiting for me, and what I become through each encounter, are processes that hinge on choice.

---

[11] From *Pilote de Guerre (1942), translated into English as Flight* to Arras. Retrieved on December 1, 2017. https://en.wikiquote.org/wiki/Antoine_de_Saint_Exupéry

Sometimes seemingly unbreakable people with seemingly unbreakable spirits are broken by circumstances. "There are no guarantees of anything in this life," I hear again and again. This is true. Yet, when the horizon appears dark, bleak and uninviting, healing happens. Spirits are raised with intention and positivity. Family and friends accept What Is, without judgment, offering sustenance and support. New light and new life awaken when we break through the unbreakable.

Day 1 of 30

44

Treatments

I started treatment today. The long quest for my best path led me here: fractionated radiation, at home, here in Toronto. And now I've begun with the best of intentions to be in a better state at the end of this six-week journey of daily zapping.

Though I didn't sleep all that well last night, feeling anticipatory jitters, the actual ordeal was not too scary. I lay on the table and the radiation technicians secured my mask. I could feel my heartbeat in my face and head, a new sensation, and probably a sign of nervousness.

The treatment didn't take long. I thought of my grandmother Carrie Saeger, who had some radiation treatments for her metastatic breast cancer over forty-five years ago. I thought of my dad, who died in 2012. I thought of the long months Earl and I have wondered what to do with my tumor and the path of discovery and decision that got me here.

Within a very few minutes, the entire procedure was done. I emerged into the waiting room doing my best zombie imitation, stumbling slowly with arms held horizontally in front. Earl scolded me for potentially scaring others in the room, but there were a few audible chuckles from more appreciative strangers. It's important to have a good sense of humor, whenever possible to do so. And if I can't laugh at Me, who can?

I'm glad to have this first step behind me now. I feel relief and a slight headache. And I'm tired. I should sleep better tonight than last.

You did well, Julie Sweet. Hang in there. (Julie Sweet is how my late grandmother Vera, whom I called Mamaw, addressed my letters and cards.)

Day 2

This was easier than the first day, because I knew what to expect and the process was completed even more quickly.

I feel fortunate, grateful to be living in this day and age when such treatment is as advanced as it is technologically and that I live in a country where my tax dollars make this available and affordable. Many generous souls give to support this hospital and all its research efforts. Though my tumor is not cancerous, I benefit from all the "cancer dollars" raised and donated. Indeed, Earl and I are proud donors every year.

My head began to ache shortly after the treatment, and during the process I was aware of the odor of the radiation. I have a very acute sense of smell.

Looking forward to resting well tonight, as I did not have the peaceful sleep I would most appreciate last night. This makes two in a row. Okay, that's my intention: I will sleep well.

You're doing great, Julie Sweet. Till tomorrow!

Day 3

I resolved to take the subway today and see if I could handle that. It went very well and I was able to walk home from my subway destination afterwards, a real treat to be outside.

All day today I felt dopey, groggier than other days. I didn't feel as headachy after the treatment though, and have not felt any nausea throughout this adventure.

Lying on the treatment table, I ask my angels, guides and Source to assist me in the best ways. I give thanks and feel all the love that others have deposited in my healthy energy bank.

We're doing super, Julie Sweet.

Day 4

The end of my first week (four days) of treatments. The treatment itself went quickly. It was a morning session because each Friday the doctor sees me; all other treatments were scheduled in the early PM.

Thursday's subway commute was preferable to car rides, as I suspected it would be. I can sit quietly and read or do a crossword puzzle and not have to be a stop-start- in-the-city car passenger. There is no smooth way to go there via car, and traffic congestion, especially like this morning's, adds another element I prefer not to have to deal with, let alone relying on others to drive.

So, hip, hip, hooray! I made it through treatment Number 4 and only 26 to go! :D

It's a weird experience being strapped down tightly by my hard mesh face mask, but the whole procedure is done so quickly, I really don't mind. In and out and back home till another day.

I can smell the radiation. That's kind of weird. I've always had a very acute sense of smell, and lo and behold, I'm one of the few who can smell it. I don't know how to describe the smell. How does one describe a smell for the first time? I'll think on that next time my tumor is "toasting." I do not taste anything. It's a very short smell, gone as soon as the radiation is done, so approximately three minutes' duration.

There is a funny little "face" (a metal box mouth and screws for eyes) on the rotating radiation machine that I greet when I am ready for zapping. I imagine my dad sitting within the little metallic face and smiling at me while I do each treatment. So funny! He had a very fine sense of humor and I carry it forward. I especially feel him with me now with each step toward healthy wholeness.

Day 10

3:30 a.m. I awoke with sharp, pounding, awful -- severe -- pain in my skull and throbbing right eye socket. It was the worst I've awakened with yet. It's still with me now almost seven hours later, though not so severe. At the time I felt Earl stir in the bed next to me, and since he was facing me I reached for his hand. He held mine firmly and, without knowing my situation, helped me through the crisis till I drifted off again. I slept off and on, but not great, till time to rise.

I've read that Buddha taught his followers that pain is inevitable, but suffering is optional. Eckhart Tolle reiterated that teaching in his books. I like that concept of pain versus suffering. Suffering is a choice. I can make other choices.

In the night, I considered medicating my pain, and I decided not to. My preference is for mental clarity, and medication further blurs that possibility, which is already a bit affected by my treatments, or so I believe. Instead, I chose to "go within" the pain and look for hidden gifts and messages.

I found a few:

- I am strong.
- I am vulnerable.
- I am one with all who are in pain.
- I am not alone.
- I am one with Source.
- I am close to all who have passed on and they are with me now. My father. My grandparents. My animals. "Hi, Motown." He was my cat.
- I am grateful.
- I know that to reach my goal (successful treatment) things may get worse before they get better.

- I accept All That Is.
- I embrace this pain and allow it to be.
- I am ready for sleep.
- I am that I AM.
- I am loved and loving.
- I find strength in my beloved Earl.
- What if everything that I experience and release can be a gift in my life?
- What if I experience this pain, release it, choose not to suffer, and find gifts inside it?

I remember two other times when I lived through very painful periods of my life, before, during and after back surgeries, and the gifts were tangible after I made it through. For one thing, I had greater compassion for myself, my physical limits, and I learned to accept help in ways that were new for me (a "do it all by myself" kind of gal before that). I also had the physical ability to carry two children, first in the womb and then in the flesh. I was able to walk and walk and walk with them, to push them in a swing set, swim with them and dance with them.

The gifts I embraced are too numerous to mention. And so it shall be again. Perhaps I'll see the gifts in everything, with practice.

I leave soon for this tenth treatment, a full two weeks since I started. I'm one-third of the way through after today. Woohoo!

*** And that was my last journal entry during the treatment process. ***

For the rest of the treatments, I managed to handle riding the subway to and from my scheduled appointments, and I did so with minimal issues. On Monday through Thursday each week, I was scheduled in the early afternoon, which made my travel easier as I avoided busy Toronto rush hour on the subway. On Fridays, I saw the radiation oncologist after my treatment, and his clinic only met in the morning, so those days required me to rise earlier and get on the subway early enough for the ride, approximately 75 minutes each way.

I enjoyed my subway rides and always brought a good book with me, a treat to be reading purely for pleasure versus doing work-oriented reading. I also enjoyed doing some jigsaw puzzle piecing while waiting in the anteroom of the radiation treatment suite. All of the support staffs were very cheerful and attentive, asking me how I was handling it all with each visit.

Once, midway through my treatments, when I had developed a nasty head and chest cold, they insisted I be seen by the doctor and quickly arranged that for the very same day. The doctor thought it wise for me to have an antibiotic to assure that I didn't grow worse. I complied with the instructions, though, for the record, I prefer not to take medication for a cold.

As the weeks of treatment rolled by, especially toward the end of the six and a half weeks, I began to notice my visual field improving in my right eye. This was very exciting, and I looked forward to an empirical confirmation of that fact when I would next see the neuro-ophthalmologist, about a month after the end of treatment.

I had been forewarned that fatigue would be a likely side effect and indeed it was! As the weeks passed I needed more and more sleep every night in order to feel alert and functional each next day. This requirement grew to about eleven hours per night, and peaked at about three weeks after the treatments concluded. It took another three weeks or so till I could get by with ten hours, another three months till nine would suffice, and almost a year till an eight-hour's rest felt sufficient for me again. I've been told the brain heals best when it is sleeping.

45

Coming Out with Outcomes

About a month post-radiation, I had a scheduled visit with the neuro-ophthalmologist, whose various tests verified what I already suspected and experienced: my right eye's vision had improved to a status of "borderline normal." Hip, hip, hooray!

I met with a headache specialist, a neurologist who took a very thorough history and then explained to me why my headaches were likely not caused by the meningioma in my brain. Apparently, there is a particular pattern most meningioma headaches follow and mine was not typical. While she could not be 100% sure of this fact, she suggested treating them as though they were migraines. And, fortunately, she had a proactive prescription for the prevention of these plaguing attacks: a tried and true medication that I now take nightly and have moderately good success taking. It took some getting used to, as I built up a tolerance to the dosage, but it's been an overall positive medication regimen. One of its beneficial side effects is deep sleep. Another, which I appreciate very much, is nerve pain relief. I have chronic issues with sciatica and tailbone pain (lingering symptoms after two low-back surgeries for spondylolisthesis). Hurray for that being better while taking this medicine to prevent migraines! I now keep a headache diary and record any issues that may arise, and I see the doctor periodically to assess this medication's efficacy.

A full six months after my radiation treatments concluded I had my next MRI scan. At this time the radiologist did not report any measurable shrinkage but did confirm there was no growth. On his own, the radiation oncologist measured some very slight shrinkage, which he showed us during our follow-up visit, and he assured us the radiologist's report was what he often saw in these circumstances: a very conservative reading.

He went on to explain that Grade 1 meningiomas grow very slowly and they also shrink and die very slowly. The DNA in each tumor cell is purposely damaged by the radiation, but it is not until the cell attempts to divide that it actually dies and shrinks away, ultimately being reabsorbed into the healthy tissue. Meningioma cell division, or growth, is a very slow process and so is the shrinkage, or death, of the tumor.

The oncologist was very encouraged by this "no growth" MRI report, and he said to expect to see a little bit of shrinkage each year going forward. My next MRI scan is scheduled for one year after the previous, and I will be followed with a yearly scan for the rest of my life.

Woohoo!

This was cause for celebration, so we did just that; and we continue to do so in many and varied ways, with deep and lasting gratitude for All That Is.

It Is What It Is:
Learning to Live with My Brain Tumor

46

Some Parting Thoughts and Helpful Resources

1. Before agreeing to radiation treatments, consider asking the doctors all the questions you wish to have answered to help inform your decision. While I have included many questions we asked my doctors, there are others you also might consider[12], including but not limited to:

- How do you protect my healthy parts from the radiation?
- What are the chances of the radiation being successful in treatment of my kind of tumor?
- Should I take vitamins, supplements and antioxidants during treatment (I was told to refrain during my treatment)?
- Should I make other changes to my usual routine, dietary or otherwise, to maximize the benefits and minimize the risks of radiation?
- Would you recommend this same treatment to your loved ones if they were in my position with my tumor?

2. I believe in the power of Alfred E. Neuman's (of *Mad Magazine* fame) catch phrase: "What Me Worry?" Many quotable sources have echoed the wisdom of letting go of worry.

- Mark Twain said, "I've had a lot of worries in my life, most of which never happened."[13]

---

[12] https://thetruthaboutcancer.com/questions-before-radiation-therapy/?gl=5828329 26&mpweb=144-1693854-421690643

[13] https://www.goodreads.com/quotes/201777-i-ve-had-a-lot-of-worries-in-my-life-most

- The Serenity Prayer: God grant me the serenity to accept the things I cannot change, the courage to change the things I can, and the wisdom to know the difference.
- Corrie ten Boom[14], whose famous book *The Hiding Place*, chronicled her family's courageous efforts to save many Jews in Holland during WWII, wrote these wise words: "Worrying does not empty tomorrow of its troubles, it empties today of its strength."
- The Buddhist rule about worrying is very simple: don't.[15]

3. Think about the story you tell yourself about yourself. We all do this every day, and especially when some dramatic change occurs in our lives. Having a brain tumor was one such change for me. What kind of story are you crafting in your mind about your role in your story? Are you the hero? Is your story an inspiring one? One of my "heroes," or people I aspire to emulate, is Leo Babauta, author of the Zen Habits blogs and books. His writing gives some simple guidance on how to be your own hero and to believe in your story in ways that make it motivate you and inspire others. I highly recommend Leo to you.[16]

4. In my experience, times of health and body challenges are great opportunities to re-examine priorities and passionately commit to oneself. As some of my writing in earlier chapters may reflect, I went through processes of prioritizing as I traversed the many roads to my eventual decision and treatment. An important lesson for me, one I am still actively learning, is How to Not Do It All. Learning to say "no" to things that aren't true priorities is the only way I know to be able to say "yes" to the things that truly are of utmost importance to me. Again, I recommend Leo Babauta's sage advice in this category of honoring oneself.[17]

5. In August 2015, President Jimmy Carter shared with the world that he had stage IV cancer. In the process of opening up with this news, our former president delivered several valuable lessons. Others, such as Stan

---

[14] https://en.wikipedia.org/wiki/Corrie_ten_Boom
[15] https://www.elephantjournal.com/2009/08/buddhist-rule-re-worrying/
[16] http://zenhabits.net/hero/
[17] https://zenhabits.net/undo/

Goldberg, MD[18], have also bravely shared their own cancer diagnosis and accompanying life lessons. I'd like to recap some of their points that resonate strongly with me. Each of them speaks to ways that we can live our lives now and thereby make our death an easier one, whenever the time comes.

- Be open and honest about your diagnosis with family and friends, or perhaps with the whole world. It takes courage to share. Doing so may greatly impact your personal and professional identity, and it may do so in ways that ultimately bring personal and professional rewards. This has been my experience.
- Carter's self-knowledge and conviction that he'd led a life of purpose helped him to calmly accept his diagnosis. I take this lesson as a prompt to make certain I am honoring priorities so that I too may know I've led a life of fulfillment. Goldberg, who serves the dying and their caregivers, asserts that living a life that made a difference is helpful to create peace at the end of life for almost everyone. In the case of my own father's end of life, it was one of the certain ways he left a legacy of love, living a life of purpose in his profession and with his family.[19]
- Think about death while your life is still ahead of you and there is time to make your desired changes. The ideal life, in my opinion, is not one of no mistakes; it is one of no regrets. Take risks. Be bold. Create and follow your dreams. Instead of worrying about whether each prospective choice will be the best for you, make the best of each choice. Prepare for death by living your chosen life. Now. And also then.
- Balance hope with reality while you continue to put one foot in front of the other. Hope is important to keep alive, as long as you are alive. It's also important to keep your perspective on what's happening with you. Finding your own balance is one key to calm acceptance and peace, at the eye of any storm you may experience.

---

[18] http://caregiving.about.com/od/endoflife/fl/Jimmy-Carterssquos-Cancer-Three-Important-Lessons.htm

[19] *Daddy, this is it. Being-with My Dying Dad*, by Julie Saeger Nierenberg. 2013. CreateWrite Enterprises. 86 pp.

6. Karen Wyatt, MD, is a physician, author and spiritual teacher whose writings and recorded interviews often inspire me and motivate me to think in new ways. Karen's article called "Why Falling Apart Is Good for You" illustrates how she finds unexpected gifts in failure and disappointment.[20] As she aptly shares, The Universe may have distinctly different plans for her than the ones she has made. I've learned this lesson many times, and am certain it will come up again in future. Karen recommends being gentle with your self when plans may seem to turn into failures. She posits that things are always falling apart, and it's not worth being upset with that fact. Learning to take life lightly helps us weather all the unexpected bumps in the road. Karen recommends learning to be grateful for the benefits of falling apart, and she has found many. These are ones that resonate strongly with me.

- You are forced to try new things and new ways of doing them.
- You learn what's top priority and commit to the steps that will reach it in the time you have.
- You can discard the habits and patterns that don't serve you well.
- You gain an appreciation for what you may have taken for granted previously.
- Your strengths and survival skills emerge as you manage to get through crises.

7. Don't get too lost in the forest when all you can see is the trees. I mentioned earlier in this book my youthful affinity for climbing trees and the comfort I feel to this day when being in their midst, communing with them on walks through the park.

There were times when I was in the midst of my discovery and decision making when I felt very oppressed, and sometimes scared, by the burdens of all there was to learn, the great volume and variance in information. And the pain in my head, which I thought was due to the tumor, was a very life-altering condition afflicting me many days and nights.

---

[20] http://www.karenwyattmd.com/apps/blog/entries/search?utf8=?&query=why+falling+apart+is+good+for+you

I remember, more than once, feeling so put-upon, I cried out, "Why me? What have I done?!" And there were a few intensely felt expletives thrown in. Who could I blame? There was no blame to place.

I was distraught and felt truly lost in the forest because I could see neither a path nor a clearing among the trees. And these "trees" felt unfamiliar and unfriendly. They were hurting me, disrupting my life, clouding my future, unsettling my peace.

And then, calling on past experience, I remembered how to "climb the tree" and get a different perspective on my grievous thoughts and concerns. I may not be certain of the path I would eventually take, but I could see, from my higher perspective, that there were paths. I could look back on old familiar walks, feel my own roots, and look forward to what may come next as a new adventure that I could embrace. I could "see the forest" with new eyes and greater acceptance.

I was not alone, right behind me and beside me were many who loved me and would care for me to the best of their ability. These too were my felt reality, not just the feeling of being lost.

There will be a way forward, for you and for me. I encourage you to embrace it. Seek solace in the trees; it's always helped me.

8. Do whatever it takes to keep your sense of humor alive and well. Laughter has healing properties and is touted to be "the best medicine."

- Watch comedy shows on TV and movies.
- Read funny books. I recommend such authors as Allen Klein[21], whose special niche genre is cultivating humor in times of health challenges and even dying times. I also love the Kliban cat comics[22] and anything by Gary Larson, the *Far Side* comedic author.[23]

---

[21] https://en.wikipedia.org/wiki/Allen_Klein_(author)
[22] http://www.eatmousies.com/html/home.html
[23] https://en.wikipedia.org/wiki/Gary_Larson

- Enroll in a Laughter Yoga (Hasyayoga) class, a practice that employs "prolonged voluntary laughter."[24] Forcing yourself to laugh will turn into real and spontaneous, usually contagious, laughter.
- Make up silly song lyrics. I did that in an earlier chapter and found lots of joy in sharing those newly revised songs with select friends.
- Choose to be with people who readily laugh and share their good cheer. The sound of laughter is the best music.
- Give your Inner Child a joyous boost by being with young children, playing, imagining, reading, holding, loving.
- Cultivate silliness. My late dad Armin was a master of All Things Silly. Silly sounds, silly looks, silly actions, silly thoughts. He "sillified" his life by choice.

9. Learn to be your own health advocate. Many have written on the topic of acquiring the skills to navigate a serious medical diagnosis. One whose writings[25] were particularly helpful to me is Elisabeth Schuler Russell, the Founder and President of Patient Navigator LLC.[26] These are some lessons I've gleaned from Elisabeth's suggestions:

- Learn as much as you can as fast as you can when you have to make decisions quickly. Health literacy is what you want to cultivate and credible sources are crucial. Learn to discern what is really valid and what is hype, both on the Internet and coming from people sources you may know.
- Document with careful note taking and/or recordings of each medical visit, diagnostic test result, etc.
- Chart your symptoms, especially if they vary, and track the factors that may have influenced them.
- Take a list of all your medications and supplements to each visit. Make a copy you can give to the doctor or nurse.
- Treat all the people you meet and greet in the medical navigation process with respect and patience. These will be your support team

---

[24] https://en.wikipedia.org/wiki/Laughter_yoga
[25] http://awomanshealth.com/serious-medical-diagnosis-start-here/
[26] http://www.patientnavigator.com/about/

and how you treat them will come back to you in kind. Learn names and contact information.

- Get all the opinions you need and want until you are satisfied you have the right one for you.
- Ask about every test or medication you are given. What does it do? Why are you taking it? What are the side effects? What should you know that you aren't asking? This is a valid question.
- Follow up if you don't hear back in a timely manner. Don't assume all will go smoothly or as expected. Take a role in making it happen.

10. Reframe your serious diagnosis as a new beginning.[27] Instead of thinking of this time as the end of your former, normal life, you can make the choice to embrace the idea of a new beginning, motivated by finding out that you have something in your life you never had before (or at least, as in my case, you didn't know you had). What can you do with this new beginning, with each new day that lies ahead? How can you make the best of the rest?

- Appreciate things you used to take for granted.
- Notice how strong you are in the face of this challenge.
- Take each day and each development one step at a time.
- Let yourself learn from your confusion; it's a great starting point.
- Choose new habits and routines that serve you better than old ones.

---

[27] http://caregiver.com/articles/print/new_normal_new_beginning.htm

EPILOGUE

At the interval of one and a half years post-radiation, my MRI shows *no growth and no shrinkage.* I still have an occasional intense headache, possibly unrelated to the tumor, and a little bit of sight change in my right eye (the side with the most optical nerve displacement). At my most recent visit with the headache specialist, she explained to me why *no growth and no shrinkage* is the very best news we could hope for. Here's why: This indicates the tumor is of the slowest growing sort and very unlikely to spread in future, because the cell turnover (when either growth or shrinkage would occur) is minimal or none at all. This result may seem counter- intuitive at first, but when she explained it to me in this detail I get it.

And I am, again, filled with gratitude.

ABOUT THE AUTHOR

Following a long career as an educator of academically gifted children in Tulsa, Oklahoma, I made a heart-led midlife leap to Toronto, Ontario. There I established myself as a freelance writer, author, editor, ghostwriter, writing coach and the Curator of Stories at CreateWrite Enterprises. These interwoven roles are my work and my passion. I feel privileged to share my perspective in the printed word and to help other authors contribute to a greater understanding of All That Is.

After publication of my personal memoir, entitled *Daddy, this is it. Being-with My Dying Dad*, in 2013, and the many and varied connections the book afforded me, I am increasingly motivated to write and speak in ways that further our cultural conversations around quality of life throughout life and unto death. I strongly believe that acceptance of death as a necessary and inevitable stage of life can enhance and enrich our daily living.

In 2017, I co-published with Victoria Brewster, MSW, a collection of perspectives from professionals and laypeople. *Journey's End: Death, Dying, and the End of Life* offers a rich variety of true stories, resources, and educational tools.

It is my hope that this current memoir, *It Is What It Is: Learning to Live with My Brain Tumor*, will also be a resource to anyone living with a difficult diagnosis, facing the decision about what treatment path to pursue and wondering how to go forward, learning to live with those choices and outcomes.

I recommend unreservedly: be transformed. From my heart to yours,
Julie Saeger Nierenberg

ALSO WRITTEN, PUBLISHED OR ILLUSTRATED BY JULIE SAEGER NIERENBERG

Journey's End: Death, Dying, and the End of Life, coauthored by Victoria Brewster and Julie Saeger Nierenberg, with contributions from many authors, 2017

Memories of Friedens: The Home of My Childhood by Armin L. Saeger and Julie Saeger Nierenberg, 2015

Our German Roots: The Turnau Family in the Time of Napoleon, A Memoir by Julia Turnau Wall and Julie Saeger Nierenberg, 2015

Daddy, this is it. Being-with My Dying Dad by Julie Saeger Nierenberg, 2013

The 1842 Diary of Julia Turnau: Sailing from Bremen to New Orleans by Julia Turnau and Julie Saeger Nierenberg, 2013

The Future Vision Map by Julie Nierenberg and Gary Evans, 2012

Sowing My Quaker Oats by Armin L. Saeger Jr., illustrated by Julie Saeger Nierenberg, 2010

Journey's End, Part 1: Heartfelt Stories of Death and Dying and Journey's End, Part 2: An Educational Guide to Death and Dying (both published in 2022)